Landing a Job
Worth Having

Vicki Lind   Tifini Roberts   Leslie Yeargers

We chose Portland's newest innovative expansion bridge, the Tilikum Crossing, as the design for our cover. The beauty of the Tilikum is enhanced by the lighting that reflects off the cables and piers, with colors fluctuating in response to the river's movement below. We've likened your job search to a new adventure, and our goal with this handbook is to create a solid structure, like the Tilikum, that can help you cross over to your new destination.

Tilikum is the Chinook word for "coming together" and conveys connection. We hope that you connect with the stories of real Portland job seekers we have helped who have successfully crossed before you.

Landing a Job Worth Having , by Vicki Lind M.S., Tifini Roberts M.S., and Leslie Yeargers M.A.

Contributors: Janet Brumbaugh, M.A., Ursala Garbrecht, and Kristin Schuchman, M.S.W.

Copyright, 2019 Portland OR.
First Edition

Editing and Production
Leslie Yeargers, M.A.

Graphic Design and Layout
Sean Yates

Copyediting/proofreading
Ben Asher

For information about Vicki Lind & Associates, please visit our website at **www.aportlandcareer.com**.

For information about Sean Yates Creative, please visit Sean's website at **www.seanyatescreative.com**.

TABLE OF CONTENTS

TABLE OF CONTENTS (Cont.)

Introduction

"The only joy in the world is to begin."
—Cesare Pavese

WELCOME TO THE JOB SEARCH ADVENTURE!

Considering that most of us spend over one-third of our life working, looking for a new job is a major undertaking. Like any new adventure, it is fraught with anticipation and excitement, as well as uncertainty. Most find the job search process deeply personal and challenging. The stresses are particularly acute if you have lost a beloved job, but they are also there if you are initiating a move to a better job.

Welcome to *Landing a Job Worth Having*. We'll help you come to a job destination that offers meaning, contribution, and balance between your family and work. This means no cookie cutter jobs, no crazy commutes, no stiff suits. We also understand that money matters because everything from a comfy home to an artisan restaurant can enhance the quality of your life.

We'll help you determine what type of job matches your current skills and knowledge, whether through traditional employment or freelance, contract, or entrepreneurial work. We're knowledgeable about Portland's employment landscape and can help you if it's time to consider relocating to other cities or countries. We take pride in staying current on today's quickly evolving tools, so we can teach you contemporary approaches to job boards, resumes, interviewing, and networking through LinkedIn. We're well equipped to guide you step-by-step to land a job that fits.

Throughout this handbook, we'll remind you that you are not alone when you are confused about which jobs to apply for, excited when you get a perfect lead, dusting yourself off after a less than perfect interview, and celebrating when you negotiate an attractive compensation package. Now is the time to set aside concerns about what lies ahead and remember:

Your Guides,

Vicki Lind, M.S.

Tifini Roberts, M.S.

Leslie Yeargers, M.A.

ABOUT THE AUTHORS

You can rest assured that our advice and guidance is grounded in the breadth of our own job-search experiences. The typical American has around ten serious jobs in their lives after college, and we hit that mark:

- Our employers have been located on the west coast, from Seattle to the Bay Area. Our recommendations are congruent with the more informal and often value-based orientation of our region. And, between the three of us, we know the Portland work scene intimately.

- We landed jobs through networking as well as by crafting effective resumes and cover letters that moved through the human resources screening process.

- Our work goals have varied during different periods of our lives. We've each had times when we held demanding professional positions: Vicki and Tifini in higher education, Tifini and Leslie in global corporations.

We also understand the entrepreneurial and creative itch, which led us to start small businesses and eventually become self-employed career professionals.

Equally important, we know the emotional terrain that goes with the job search adventure. At times, like you, we were catapulted to new career heights by the excitement of reaching the next peak. Other times, we were anxious...running out of money, scared we would not find a job, or both. When facing new challenges, we armed ourselves with the best knowledge and the best guides to achieve our goals. Now, it is our turn to joyfully pass on our personal and professional wisdom.

VICKI LIND, M.S.

Vicki's Formal Qualifications

I hold a master's degree in education from Portland State University, Oregon, and a master's degree in counseling psychology from the University of Oregon. A lifelong learner, I later completed the coursework for a certificate in human resource management from Linfield College, Oregon.

Vicki's Colorful Career Path

One of my greatest interests in life has been learning about the stages of human development throughout the life span. I believe that our twenties are a time for getting a broad education through both study and bold exploration—from studying poetry to traveling to India to playing in a band. Clients in their early thirties often tell me that they feel "behind" their friends who went straight through medical school, law school, etc. They can take heart from my own colorful, varied twenties. Before I was 30, I had the following jobs:

- Picked strawberries, babysat and was a camp counselor (Portland, OR)

- Created a neighborhood newspaper, The Taylor's Ferry Herald (Portland, OR)

- Sold overpriced alligator purses on Fifth Avenue (New York, NY)

- Planned programs in a camp for Hispanic mothers and children (Chicago, IL)

- Picked peaches (Israel)

- Helped in a camp for homeless people (France)

- Assisted in day treatment for the mentally ill (San Francisco, CA)

- Temped (San Francisco, CA)

- Taught at a day care center for African-American children (Oakland, CA)

- Mothered Jessica and Miriam; lived on a commune (Mist, OR)

- Worked as a Fire Watch (Mist, OR)

- Sold crafts at craft fairs (Portland, OR)

- Finished my first master's degree in education, putting down my first serious career roots

- Became Head Start Education Coordinator (Clatskanie and Astoria, OR)

- Taught parenting classes at Clatsop County Mental Health (Astoria, OR)

- Taught Early Childhood Education and Psychology at Clatsop Community College (Astoria, OR)

- After six years, I became more interested in how adults grow and transform themselves, using education as a tool. I admired the bravery and tenacity I saw in adults who decided to open new doors by finishing their education. I also woke up to the merits of health insurance and retirement planning and plunged seriously into a commitment to the following long-term positions:

- Student Advisor for Linfield College (Albany, OR and Astoria, OR)

- Director of Adult Degree Program, Linfield College (McMinnville, OR)

I was very successful for the first decade, followed by a few years of searing burnout, which culminated in being asked to resign. I insisted that they throw me a big celebratory good-bye party. I enjoyed the validation, but my leaving was followed by a period of pain and confusion. I share this because I have found that doing so has helped scores of talented professionals who also have had a mixed bag of successful and painful career experiences.

I wanted to get it right for my third career. I read career books and identified my top skills as facilitating groups, connecting people with resources and coaching/counseling individuals. I clarified what I valued: variety, autonomy, creativity, and flexibility to make time to garden and create art. Then, I identified three options that seemed to match: diversity trainer, mediator, and career counselor. I took six months to try out what I now label "strategic volunteering" and career counseling won handily!

"Leadership requires chutzpah." —Vera Katz

TIFINI ROBERTS, M.S.

Tifini's Formal Qualifications

I hold a Master of Science degree in communication studies from Portland State University and take resume writing and strategy courses through multiple national resume writers' organizations. A self-proclaimed "research geek," I enjoy keeping current on ever-changing resume practices and dedicate myself to continuing my education regularly.

TIFINI'S CAREER PATH

My path to resume writing and career services was long and winding. Growing up in the Portland Metro area I had the opportunity and connections to work as an in-house temporary employee at a large local bank right out of high school. Eventually hired full-time in several administrative positions, each increasing in responsibility, I decided banking was not my calling. During this time, I was also in the United States Navy Reserves as a Hospital Corpsman.

I moved around working for a women-owned government contractor as a visual writer and graphic designer, a small start-up for ground-breaking medical devices, and finally ended up in graduate school as a full-time student and part-time college instructor. After graduate school I volunteered at a nonprofit, which turned into a full-time gig as the program and development manager, and simultaneously started a glass art and jewelry business. Eventually, I missed teaching and education and took a position at a local community college to run a large program and teach courses in communications.

Still not convinced I found my calling, I started the long process of identifying my strengths and passions. While reflecting on what was most important to me and what I had to offer, I connected with Vicki Lind. From our conversations, resume writing and career services emerged as a perfect combination of my strengths, experiences, education, and most of all, desire to help people achieve their own goals.

Soon after I launched my own career services business focused on resume writing, Vicki reached out to me to join her team as their resume writer. The timing was serendipitous, and the opportunity was a fantastic fit. The moral of my story is keep networking, learning, and trying new things. You never know who will offer you a job or where you will be able to apply your knowledge and skills.

"Never give in." —Winston Churchill

LESLIE YEARGERS, M.A.

Leslie's Formal Qualifications

I hold a Bachelor of Art degree in German and a self-designed minor in technical communication from the University of Michigan. I later returned to school to earn a Master of Arts degree in Applied Behavioral Science from the Leadership Institute of Seattle (LIOS) program at Bastyr University. My focus was on family systems counseling and I am a licensed Marriage and Family Therapist intern. I am also a certified hypnotherapist in addition to being formally trained as a job search coach.

Leslie's Career Adventure

My career adventure has not been on a straight and level path; it has included a few uphill climbs, downhill slopes, hard-angle turns, and 180-degree pivots.

When I started college at the University of Michigan, I wanted to be a doctor. My sophomore year I discovered I possessed a complete and utter lack of aptitude for organic chemistry, so I made a right-angle turn and decided to get my degree in German—great plan for graduating, not so great for developing a solid career path, so I worked with the engineering department to devise a personalized technical writing program and internship. After graduation, my career adventure took me to Düsseldorf, Germany where I worked as a localizer/translator for a software company.

When I returned to the states I continued on what I thought would be a straight and narrow career path in technical writing. I took an independent contractor position at Microsoft. After a couple of years working independently, I signed on with a temporary agency and then eventually became a full-time Microsoft employee.

After five years of technical writing working at a breakneck pace under tight deadlines, I was totally burnt out. I made an abrupt hard-angle turn and went back to school to earn a Master's degree in Applied Behavioral Sciences. I had found my passion—I quit Microsoft so that I could devote my energy and time to my studies and an internship at a family services agency where I counseled couples, families, and teenage girls.

Two and half years later and tens of thousands of dollars in the hole, I took a 180-degree turn back in the direction from whence I came, landing full circle once again as a technical writer at Microsoft. Not ready to dismiss two years of counseling training, I worked nights as a cotherapist in a therapy group and ran my own private practice as a registered counselor in the State of Washington. I also picked up a hypnotherapy certification to add to my counseling tool kit.

About two years into my third stint at Microsoft, I was offered an employee relations job by my temp agency. Without hesitation I took this fork in the road. The opportunity to combine counseling skills with technical writing skills and a knowledge of Microsoft's departments, managers, and corporate culture was too good an adventure to pass up. Landing that job was like running downhill—the opportunity was custom designed for my skill set and it happened quickly with great ease.

When my children were born I did what a lot of women do: I got off the well-trodden career path and entered the uncharted twisty turning roads of the stay-at-home parent. For 15 years I followed the winding paths of various volunteer activities that revolved around my kids: classroom helper, school PTA boards, booster boards, fund-raisers, and a long and intense involvement with the Rock 'n' Roll Camp for Girls. I took up the electric bass and joined a couple bands.

As my kids got older and needed less of my time and more of our money—or rather my husband's money, because although I was busy developing what I hoped were marketable skills, I had not earned an income in over 13 years—it was time to get back onto the career path. I went back to school to become eligible for licensure as a Marriage and Family Therapist in Oregon. I embarked upon a steep uphill climb of looking for paid internships and an approved supervisor. Along the way I came to a much-needed downhill slope when a friend alerted me to a receptionist job in a real estate office. I took the job, earned my real estate license, and started a career as an assistant for a team at a quintessential Portland real estate brokerage firm. I hated it and was not very good at it. After three months I was released from that job and found myself, once again, unemployed.

I hadn't given up on my dream of working as a counselor, in social services, or as a career professional in an HR-related job, so I decided it was time for some strategic volunteering. I became a court-appointed special advocate (CASA). Shortly after that, I saw an announcement on Mac's List for a position at Vicki Lind & Associates. The thought of making a 180-degree turn back into career services was most appealing! I've been at Vicki Lind & Associates for two and half years, applying my skills to intake counseling, resume writing, job search and interview coaching, newsletter writing, book writing and editing, website content updates, and whatever else I can do to support the business.

After several years of uphill climbs, abrupt turns, and a few downhill reprieves, I've finally landed my dream job in Portland. I have no doubt that you will too!

"Find out what you like doing best, and get someone to pay you for it."
—Katherine Whitehorn

ABOUT THIS HANDBOOK

You've picked up this handbook because you are not happy with your current job or career. The reasons are legion. Maybe you have:

- Graduated from college and can't land a job related to your major.

- Had a successful job and are now bored—you are ready for novelty.

- A negative boss who is scarce with praise and rich with criticism.

- A compensation package that doesn't match your contribution.

- Been asked to relocate and you don't want to move.

- Been working evenings and weekends and your life is out of balance.

- Please fill in other reasons that you are ready for new employment:

_____

_____

_____

Maybe you are unemployed and have been sending resumes into the void. You may not know how to handle things like:

- Gaps in your work history.

- Understanding the new technology that screens resumes.

- Current trends in resume writing.

- How to interview effectively.

- Ageism and other discrimination.

- Please fill in other concerns you have about finding a new job that you like:

_____

_____

_____

IS THIS HANDBOOK FOR YOU?

*If you have a dream of securing a new job in a new industry using new skills, this is not the handbook for you. This type of career makeover is called "Career Transition" and is covered in the companion handbook **Finding a Career Worth Having**, a book that was originally written by Vicki Lind and Cynthia Dettman.*

Finding a Career Worth Having *was written initially to help career changers and job seekers go through a do-it-yourself process to transition into new careers and then find their dream jobs. Because the world of job search is ever-changing, Vicki kept releasing new editions, adding content to stay current. By the fourth edition, the job search section in Finding a Career... had grown by 50 percent and the book was bursting at the seams. Plus, while there are some common steps and elements to both, the needs of career transitioners and job seekers are different. Vicki thought, "Why not break up the book into two separate books, one for career exploration and transition and one for job search?" Thus, **Landing a Job worth Having** was born.*

*In the next version of **Finding a Career...** (planned release in 2019) we will take you through a career transition process comprised of in-depth self-assessment and thorough career exploration, followed by education and training for the new career. On average, it takes a year or two to acquire new skills and enter a new career.*

HOW WE ORGANIZED THIS HANDBOOK

When you embark on a serious adventure, you need to have a reliable GPS system or road map (for those of us who are still a little old-school) to help you navigate the winding streets, right-angle turns, and hilly terrain. Think of this handbook as your job search navigation system; we'll guide you on your job search adventure, offering practical suggestions, tips, and advice as well as support and reassurance when the going gets tough. We stay with you every step of the way!

In *Get Ready for the Adventure* we get you off to a good start. We offer tips and tools to help you not only survive the job search adventure, but to enjoy it and thrive during the experience. You'll learn about the tools you need—from supportive friends and family to technical skills—to be successful in reaching your final destination...a job you love!

Once you are prepared, we lead you through a seven-step process to finding a job worth having. We begin with **Step 1: Clarify Your Job Goals—What Do You Want?** In this section we help you determine the criteria important to you in a job and an employer. We show you how to research different jobs and companies so that you know where to look when you search for job postings, which naturally leads you to **Step 2: Find Position Openings—Who Wants You?** In this section we show you how to use job boards and social media to find postings that match your criteria. We also talk about internships and how to design your own as well as address special considerations for those of us who are 50 or better.

After finding that perfect position announcement, we take you through **Step 3: Prepare Your Resume and Cover Letter**. We show you how to craft a resume that will outsmart application tracking software so that your resume will rise to the top of the heap and win you an interview. We also show you how to write a cover letter that will get the attention of even the most discerning hiring manager.

When on a serious adventure it's a good idea to use the buddy system for support and security. In terms of job search this means connecting with others who can help and put in a good word. In **Step 4: Find Your Networking Style** we help you develop a networking strategy that matches your personality. We also get your LinkedIn presence in tip-top shape so you can develop those online relationships that can be most influential in your job search.

For many, interviewing is the most anxiety-ridden leg of the job search adventure. In **Step 5: Interview with Confidence** we help alleviate interview stress by making sure you are well-prepared. We offer practical information from common questions to advice on what to wear, and we address special interview challenges for the older and overqualified candidate.

In **Step 6: Gather Your References** we describe how to make sure you are getting the best references possible and what to do if you think you might get some that are not so good. When all your hard work has finally paid off and you are presented a job offer, it is essential to know how to negotiate your compensation package. In **Step 7: Negotiate and Accept the Job** we show you how to do just that.

We offer *Gifts to Give Yourself* at crucial points on your adventure because treating yourself with little rewards for accomplishing difficult tasks is an important aspect of self-care. We want you to stay motivated and engaged when you encounter twists, turns, and uphill climbs.

OTHER ADVENTURERS' STORIES

Most of you know clearly what you do not want in your next job and have glimmers of what would work better. Some of our clients, who have given us permission to use their real names, have been on the same job search adventure as you. Here is how theirs started. If you are curious, you might want to flip to the last article in the handbook, *Conclusion: Saying "Yes!"*, to find out how their adventures ended.

Andrea Gomez came to us as a single mother, exhausted by braiding together gigs as a barista and Airbnb photographer. She loved Portland culturally, but struggled to make ends meet with the rising rents. Financial stability using her creative and organizational skills was her goal.

Nancy Banes had taken time off from her career as an environmental engineer. Now that her kids were in high school, she wanted to return to her career. She was concerned about the impact of the 17-year gap when she focused on parenting and volunteering for a robotics team.

Another client, who wished to remain anonymous, moved to Portland from Israel to support his wife's desire to further her career at Intel. While he had an MBA, combined with a solid engineering and web development background, his resume wasn't congruent with current American standards.

Laura Belson had a string of volunteer jobs after college, without any specific focus. She needed to highlight her top skills in her resume to aim for a paying, entry-level position with heart.

Mariann Hyland wanted to advance her career and obtain a top-level leadership position in which she could maximize her impact on diversity, equity, and inclusion. To reach her goal she needed a standout LinkedIn presence combined with a compelling resume that highlighted her achievements.

Dawn Hampton was Vicki's barista at Starbucks. She had stepped away from her earlier career in human resources management and was trying to return to it. She came to us after sending out many resumes without any responses.

Like you, these folks had a mix of valuable knowledge and skills and often some bruising and doubts from past employment. They also felt overwhelmed by a long and conflicting list of what-to-do and common mistakes that people make in today's changed job search market. By working with us and following the recommendations in this book, they eventually achieved success. With this trusted guide in hand, you will too—turn to *Get Ready* and let's get started!

"Be positive, patient and persistent." —Bansky

Get Ready for the Adventure

"Every single journey that I've embarked on, I've learned something new." —Shailene Woodley

While on your job search adventure, you'll probably vacillate between periods of excitement when new possibilities arise and periods of emotional upheaval and doubts. Job seekers rarely talk about these negative feelings publicly because it is important to show a positive face when networking. If you are unsatisfied in your current position, you may have to pretend that you still find selling socks meaningful. Or, if you're unemployed, you may hate being constantly asked how the search is going. You may say, breezily, "I'm enjoying spending quality time with the kids, and there are several interesting options that I am exploring." You might wish you could groan deeply and say frankly, "I am binge watching *Mad Men* for the third time."

This section helps you prepare in ways much like getting ready for a new adventure. The first task is to consider your emotional preparation: identifying, for instance, frightening unknowns. To offset any emotional challenges it is important to assess your resources, review your self-care needs, and stay in contact with those who provide positive support or fun respite when you feel worn down.

Our first article, *Surviving and Thriving*, introduces you to several tools to help you identify practical and technical items you'll need for a successful job search. In addition to the practical stuff, this article prompts you to consider your emotional needs and challenges while undertaking the job search adventure. The second article, *Pack Your Tool Bag*, organizes these tools into a handy checklist to identify and track your preparations.

The final article, *Build Technical and Social Media Skills*, will motivate you to improve critical technical skills so that you will be current and competitive in your field. We also emphasize creating or improving your LinkedIn profile because most prospective employers seriously considering you will look you up on LinkedIn.

If you are currently employed, we understand that you won't have time to implement all of the tools; you will need to determine which ones are most relevant to your unique job search adventure. If you are unemployed, we encourage you to dive deeper into this section, returning to it to add more tools and refine others to hone your readiness and gain momentum. Happy Trails!

SURVIVING AND THRIVING

Some experts claim that job seeking is a full-time job. We disagree. We think it is an excellent time to develop a schedule that balances job-seeking tasks at the computer, enjoyable networking, skill building, self-care, and pleasure. It is also a wonderful time to engage in physical, spiritual, and social play that won't fit as easily into your schedule after you have a job.

We created the checklist *Pack Your Tool Bag* on the next page to help start your job search with a positive mindset. The checklist has four categories of tools: practical elements that support your search, technology and social media tools you'll want to consider learning, elements of spiritual/emotional support, and means for engagement in community. These are discussed briefly here.

PRACTICAL ELEMENTS

We start the checklist with practical tools, particularly the importance of creating and stocking an attractive area in which to work. Vicki's father, a small-business consultant, advised, "You'll work best with a clean desk that only includes three items: your immediate task, a picture of someone you love, and something living...like a plant or goldfish."

TECHNOLOGY TOOLS

Being up-to-date on the latest software and social media trends can be most beneficial to your job search. Do you want to brush up on Google Docs or Microsoft Office? We highly recommend engaging in social media, especially LinkedIn, to research jobs and employers as well as network with other professionals who share your desired job title or work at your target company. Now is the time to hone your expertise with these tools.

SPIRITUAL/EMOTIONAL SUPPORT

We next turn to tools that will strengthen you internally and help you invite joy, peace, and meaning into your process. It is a time to review the tools that have helped you through other life challenges—from journaling to golf. It is a time to find and strengthen your connections to people who can both share the inside journey and support the outward tasks of the search.

In addition to supportive family and friends, you might consider working with a job search coach and/or resume writer. We can help you clarify your employment must-haves, overcome doubts and fears, and provide practical tools such as resume and interview help. Almost all of us provide at least a free 15-minute phone consultation and have personal websites. Some of you may sense already that your progress will be faster and more sure-footed with professional help in designing your job search plan. Minimally, it's time to call when you have tried your own strategies and feel stuck.

COMMUNITY ENGAGEMENT

If you are unemployed, you may have lost the community of coworkers you engaged with on a daily basis. Belonging to communities—even taking time to meet your neighbors—provides support at a challenging time. Community engagement also provides networking opportunities that are integral to the successful job search.

Now it's time to pack your tool bag and get underway!

Written by Vicki Lind and Kristin Schuchman

Reflect on each tool and select an action item that fits your style and schedule. Then, review your list and assign a number from 1 to 4 with 1 being the highest priority and 4 being the lowest. Finish by transferring your most important action items to your calendar or "to do" list.

If you are employed full-time, choose a few that will have the most impact. If you are unemployed, you have the luxury of spending more time on skill building and taking care of your emotional and social life. Clip or dog-ear this page so you can return to repack your bags, if needed, until you receive that hot job offer.

TOOLS	Action	Priority Rank
1. PRACTICAL TOOLS		
Inviting work area		
Dedicated workspace		
Do Not Disturb conversation/sign		
File and folder system		
Financial review		
Locate old resume(s)		
Other:		
2. TECHNOLOGY TOOLS		
Software skills		
LinkedIn and social media		
Update and engage contacts		
Calendar app		
Other		
3. SPIRITUAL/EMOTIONAL TOOLS		
Books and movies		
Podcasts		
Dates with friends		
Creative expression		
Getaways		
Career counselor/job search		
Other		
4. COMMUNITY ENGAGEMENT		
Professional associations		
Strategic volunteering		
Spiritual affiliation		
Meetups		
Other		

1. PRACTICAL ELEMENTS

Inviting work area – Set up an office area and make it a place where you want to spend time. Decorate with plants, motivational quotes, or pictures of loved ones.

Dedicated workspace – Create a space that will allow you to work without interruption, preferably a place where you can close the door and work quietly and store materials.

***Do Not Disturb* conversation/sign** – If you are unemployed, everyone will assume that you are now available to mow the lawn, pick up your brother-in-law from the airport, and cheerfully make time for every errand. Talk to people in your life to let them know that you must commit focused time to your job search. Make it clear when you are not to be disturbed. If you have a dedicated space with a door, you might want to hang a *Do Not Disturb* sign on the door handle.

File and folder system – Develop an information-storage system with clear labels for easy access. If you like to have things on paper, you can create a binder or series of folders, one for each section of this handbook. In addition to saving position announcements and resume drafts, you can collect articles and links to resources that inform and energize your job search.

Financial review – If you are unemployed, you need to review your finances and possibly make tough decisions. Do I need to cancel our vacation? Should I tap emergency funds to find the ideal job? Can I work part-time while I search for a job? Do I have relatives or friends to tap if things get tight? If you have a spouse or partner, set aside time for a discussion about money matters. Imagine your most comfortable job search journey with a quick and soft landing to a great destination. Also develop a plan B

for a less direct route to employment. After reviewing the facts, set a salary goal as well as the lowest amount you are willing to accept if other factors, such as benefits and vacation time, are ideal.

Locate old resumes – Don't worry too much about polishing your resume just yet, but do dig up your latest version—as well as positive performance reviews—so that they are easily accessible when needed. Add your most recent position to your resume if you have not done so already. Reviewing your resumes may also remind you of your accomplishments and boost your confidence.

2. TECHNOLOGY TOOLS

Software skills – Now is the time to take your Google Docs and Microsoft Office skills to the next level. Many websites offer clear step-by-step computer training (see *Build Technical and Social Media Skills* for a list). If you prefer a brick-and-mortar classroom setting, community colleges and workforce centers offer free and low cost- training. If it's relevant to your job goal, add a database program or specialized software program. If you are in a creative field, improve your portfolio while building skills in the Adobe Creative Suite programs.

LinkedIn and social media – Because 93 percent of hiring managers use LinkedIn and a staggering number of people (over two billion as of January 2018) are using Facebook, it makes sense to join the bandwagon so your network can assist you in your job search. See *Facebook for Job Search* and *LinkedIn for Job Research* to learn more.

Update and engage contacts – You will be tapping your colleagues and friends in many ways—from providing leads to offering comfort when you blow an interview. Before you start making requests, touch base with your key connections and supporters. If you have a drawer full of business cards from events

Written by Vicki Lind and Kristin Schuchman

you've attended, update your email, social media, and LinkedIn contact lists.

Calendar app – If you do not have an effective electronic calendar application in place, prioritize this activity. We like Google Calendar, but Microsoft Outlook and Apple's iCal are also popular. Whether you go high-tech or old-school with a paper planner, be sure to block out time for self-care, reflection, coffee dates, and getaways.

3. SPIRITUAL/EMOTIONAL TOOLS

Books and movies – Most heroes and heroines show grit and resolve when overcoming obstacles to fulfilling their dreams. By engaging in their stories, we become inspired and muster our courage and motivation to confront our own barriers. Vicki and Leslie were inspired by watching *RBG*, the story of how Ruth Bader Ginsberg overcame serious odds (as well as two bouts with cancer) to serve on the Supreme Court. Tifini gains inspiration by watching movies and reading books based on true stories of inspiration where the underdog prevails, such as the film *The Blind Side* and the book *The Girl with No Name*.

Podcasts – These are great for expanding your horizons while doing the dishes or walking the dog. Vicki was surprised to learn from *Eat, Pray, Love* author Elizabeth Gilbert that following your passion, while perfect in some cases, can have serious unintended consequences. Leslie loves listening to NPR's Radiolab with her husband while driving their daughter to college in Boulder, Colorado. She discovers new technologies, learns about obscure current events, and hears a variety of perspectives on timely topics.

Dates with friends – This is something we don't always think to chisel into our schedules, especially if we're spending a lot of time at home. Make time for friends and don't hesitate to ask for their help and insights about you. You may discover some pleasant surprises!

Getaways – We are big fans of road trips, but if this proves impossible, little day trips are invaluable at this time to relax and expand your thinking. Take yourself to those places that offer mindful appreciation of the world and provide a psychological reboot. Vicki's favorite spots include the wetlands of Sauvie Island and Manzanita; Leslie enjoys exploring Tryon Creek and taking urban walks in different Portland neighborhoods. Tifini, who lives on a rustic mountaintop, enjoys getaways to the beach where she can walk along the shoreline and hike the coastal range.

Creative expression – You do not need to be a Picasso or virtuoso pianist to express yourself creatively. Creative expression could be as simple as keeping a brief diary or singing in the shower—both of which are shown to have therapeutic benefits. Ignoring your creative side can lead to depression and anxiety, especially if you need creative expression to feel like a human. During tough times Vicki makes *Soul Collage Cards* on topics such as endurance and acceptance. Leslie raises her voice with others in the Portland Interfaith Gospel Choir and plays bass guitar in a band with her husband. Tifini gets out her bead collection to craft beautiful gifts for others.

Career counselor/job search coach – Your friends and family can help you only to a point. When it's time for skilled assistance with a robust, contemporary job search, a career counselor or job search coach can provide expert guidance.

4. COMMUNITY ENGAGEMENT

Professional associations – Attending networking groups and the meetings of professional associations is a great way to make contacts and learn more about different job titles, companies, and self-employment options. When you attend, collect business cards and then follow up by connecting on LinkedIn or other social media. If you had a particularly good connection, set up a coffee date.

Strategic volunteering – Nonprofits, professional associations, and civic organizations are constantly looking for people to help with marketing, social media, events, and community outreach. Volunteer for tasks that build your skills or give you the opportunity to meet professionals in your field.

Spiritual affiliation – If you have a place of worship, consider ways to deepen your involvement. Reach out to more members of your spiritual community and engage in practices that will bolster your spirit during challenging periods. You may find kindred spirits add strength in nontraditional settings such as a martial arts studio, a hiking club, or a 12-Step group.

Meetups – Whatever your interest, there is a meetup for you. You can attend meetups to practice and improve a certain skill (for example, Spanish at Lunch) or you can connect with other professionals at meetups like Portland Wellness Practitioners or Beers with Engineers. Of course, you can choose a meetup to foster a hobby, for emotional vitalization through creativity, or just for convening with others in nature (The Meditation, Joy, and Tea Meetup is one of the hundreds to choose from).

Work steadily on this checklist but don't let its lack of completion keep you from moving forward. You can take practical steps in your job search while using and building on the tools you think are helpful. We want you to take advantage of your internal momentum as it builds!

"Take what you can use and let the rest go by." —Ken Kesey

> **Tip**
>
> *You don't need to use all the tools—that could be a bit overwhelming. You know what tools will serve you best*

BUILD TECHNICAL AND SOCIAL MEDIA SKILLS

Like it or not, the technological revolution has had a major impact on how we work and personally interact. As of January 2018, 467 million people are on LinkedIn, the foremost professional social media site with over 11 million active job listings. While the pressure to engage in social media platforms can feel oppressive, it helps to remember that there is a platform for everyone.

Think of social media platforms as some of the stranded passengers on Gilligan's Island—LinkedIn is the Professor, stately and a little stiff but very intelligent; Twitter is the Skipper, all goofiness but little self-awareness; Gilligan is Facebook, the bungling yet loveable linchpin of the group, bringing everyone together but often giving you ample cause to throw him off the island; Ginger is Instagram, glamorous and lovely to look at but not likely to hold a conversation for long; and Pinterest is Mary Ann, conventionally useful in many ways and always cheerfully creative. (Sorry that we didn't fit you into the metaphor, Mr. and Mrs. Howell, but the world isn't quite ready for a social media platform suited to you.)

Note: As of this writing Facebook, with 2.13 billion members and counting, is the winner and is starting to dip its toe into the recruiting world by listing job postings. It remains to be seen if this new feature will take hold, but it seems likely Facebook could capture a market of people for whom LinkedIn holds little or no appeal.

NOW IS THE TIME TO BUILD YOUR SKILLS

You may be hesitant to spend time on building technical skills, believing that you are a fast learner able to master these skills after you are hired. This belief may be buoyed by managers who say that communication skills and critical thinking abilities play a larger role in their hiring decisions than specific technical skills that can be learned. Such comments often mislead job applicants to apply to jobs for which they do not have the required technical skills.

Keep in mind the resume screeners are the gatekeepers and tend to be more concrete and literal than the managers. In fact, over 80 percent of midsized and larger companies use applicant tracking software (ATS) to score resumes based on keywords and technical skills (for more information, see *Applicant Tracking Software* in **Step 3: Plan Your Resume and Cover Letter**). Only a small subset of those that make it through the system—those that best match the qualifications for years of experience and technical skills—are presented to the hiring manager. Managers then make their more holistic assessment based on interpersonal and other soft skills.

In short, unless you have some well-developed pipelines to hiring managers, use time during your job search to upgrade your technical skills.

FIND THE RIGHT ENVIRONMENT

Begin by reflecting on what kind of environment will help you achieve optimal mental clarity so that you can stick to the task of building your technical skills. If you've experienced resistance in the past, explore this task as a learning experiment. Try something new, like inviting your computer-obsessed nephew over to help you learn and grasp social media. Notice if this process was enjoyable and productive for you. If not, try something else...maybe a workshop.

FACTORS THAT INCREASE SUCCESS	Helpful	Somewhat Helpful	Not Helpful
Working at home			
Working at a coffee shop			
Working alongside a friend			
Online courses and tutorials			
Classes/workshops (in-person)			
Help from technologically-savvy friend or relative			
Blocking out regular time in your calendar			
Other:			

RESOURCES TO BUILD YOUR TECHNOLOGY SKILLS

If you need help assessing your level of competency and creating a structure for training, we've found these sites to be extremely friendly, affordable, and effective:

- **LinkedIn.com/Learning** (formerly **Lynda.com**) has 63,000 video tutorials, from basic to advanced skill levels. Topics include audio, business, design, photography, video, web + interactive and more. For a basic fee you can determine your current level and use as many tutorials as you like. Training is broken down into microlessons, so you can learn in ten-minute bites or focus on a course for several hours.

- **Office.com** offers free training and troubleshooting tutorials for all Microsoft products in the form of videos and downloadable PDFs. Microsoft also offers a wide range of certification trainings through third-party vendors for a fee. These certifications can help you develop skills for positions in administration and project management as well as add to your qualifications for any career.

- **TeamTreehouse.com** can help you build your programming skills for a fraction of the price of formal computer education classes. Acquire specialized training in tools like Javascript and Python and even earn certifications you can put on your resume. **Udacity.com**, **OReilly.com**, and **LearnToProgram.tv** offer similar services.

Written by Kristin Schuchman

Coursera.com offers over 2,000 courses and certificates from schools like Stanford and Yale. Build career skills in data science, computer science, and business. Most are free and feature feedback from other course participants.

Assessing and building technical and social media skills can feel like a daunting task, especially if the technical/ social media train has left you behind at the station. Now is a great time to take a break and refresh.

 HERE ARE A FEW GIFTS TO GIVE YOURSELF TO HELP YOU REFRESH

- *Take an afternoon nap.*

- *Treat yourself to a relaxing massage.*

- *Draw a picture, even if you don't think you can, or try an adult coloring book--they are quite relaxing.*

- *Take a walk in your favorite neighborhood or park and see if you notice something new.*

- *Visit Powell's and pick out a good novel. Order your favorite beverage in their cafe and enjoy your new find.*

- *Read about someone whose life had purpose or changed our world. Examples include Rachel Ignotofsky's* **Women in Science**, *Walter Isaacson's* **Steve Jobs,** *or Ron Chernow's* **Hamilton.**

- *Visit a tourist site or historic building in your city. In Portland, we like our downtown library and aerial tram. If you live in a rural area, make a trip to the big city, or go on a tour of vintage barns.*

JOB SEARCH CHECKLIST

When you consider the entire job search process it is easy to get overwhelmed. That's why we've developed the following checklist. It helps clients break up their job search into manageable tasks.

I. IDENTIFY EMPLOYER/JOB CHARACTERISTICS

❏ Where could the employer be located? _____

❏ Which sector or industry? _____

❏ What is your desired salary range? _____

❏ What schedule do you want to work? How many hours? _____

❏ Does it need to have health benefits? _____

❏ What is most important to you in the work culture? _____

❏ Any other traits must the job or employer have? _____

❏ Who is part of your support system? _____

❏ Identify possible job titles and/or keywords that match your current skills and expertise.

1. _____ 3. _____

2. _____ 4. _____

II. RESEARCH JOB TITLES AND LOCATE POSITION ANNOUNCEMENT

❏ Learn to use **Indeed** to locate appropriate position announcements.

❏ Use **LinkedIn's** Jobs search function.

❏ Identify **additional job sites** most likely to post in your field and review regularly.

1. _____ 3. _____

2. _____ 4. _____

❏ Research **desirable employers** (you can list up to 20 on another piece of paper)

1. _____ 6. _____

2. _____ 7. _____

3. _____ 8. _____

4. _____ 9. _____

5. _____ 10. _____

III. PREPARE RESUME AND LINKEDIN PROFILE

❑ Target your first **resume** to a specific job announcement, using keywords and requirements.

❑ Write your first compelling **cover letter**.

❑ Create a **LinkedIn profile**.

IV. CHOOSE A NETWORKING STYLE

❑ Create a **basic message** for in-person networking that identifies what you are seeking.

❑ Stay in touch with **connections** in your network who may hear of job openings.

❑ Get to know your **targeted employers** by networking with past or current employees.

❑ **Volunteer** and/or **intern** strategically to build contacts in your field.

❑ Join and participate in **professional organizations or groups** that match your career objective(s). Consider a mix of live meetings and LinkedIn groups.

V. APPLY AND INTERVIEW CONFIDENTLY

❑ **Customize each resume**, especially the profile and keywords at the top for each job posting.

❑ **Customize each cover letter** and align your skills with the employer's needs.

❑ **Contact LinkedIn connections** who may know the decision makers in the company.

❑ **Develop CAR (Challenge, Action, Results) stories** to use in the interview.

❑ **Practice interviewing**.

Step 1
Clarify Your Job Goals:
What Do You Want?

"I thought I was going to make crazy cartoons for the rest of my life. I didn't think I'd ever get paid for it, didn't think I drew well enough, but I knew it made me happy." —Matt Groening

If you don't know where you are going, you'll end up somewhere else," according to Yogi Berra. In job search terms, this means that you need to figure out where you want to ultimately end up on your job search adventure. Otherwise, you could end up with a new job you hate, and once again have to get out of Dodge. In this section, we'll help you define your destination, from your ideals to the trade-offs that you would find acceptable. We'll help you clarify what you want while staying tethered to practical realities. Then, you can begin the process of seeing what jobs are out there to find positive and realistic matches.

In ***What Matters to You***, we'll guide you to drill down to consider practical matters, such as specific location and concrete financial needs, as well as factors that will give your days meaning and a sense of contribution.

As you assess what matters to you, it may become clear that you don't want to have long-term, traditional 9-to-5 employment, particularly if it requires an uncomfortable commute. The world of work is rapidly changing and now offers self-employment alternatives, ranging from year-long on-site contract work to remote freelance opportunities. In ***Is Self-Employment for You***, we'll introduce you to this new work landscape and help you determine if you have the characteristics necessary to be self-employed.

Figuring out what you want in a job is essential, but your ideas need to be grounded in jobs that are actually out there. What is realistic and what is a stretch? You might want to know if you can apply your sales skills in technology to an industry you love, like beer or travel. By following our guidelines in ***LinkedIn for Job Research***, you'll see the types of employers and job titles that are available to people with your background and skill set.

We encourage every job seeker to identify and follow about twenty potential employers to determine if they are a good fit for what matters to you. In ***Identify Target Employers***, you'll be introduced to the best tools to learn about employers, particularly the inside scoop from their current and past employees.

Many of our clients begin the process of homing in on their ideal job criteria by saying they are "all over the place." By the end of Step 1, your career destination will come into clearer focus; you'll be able to make heartfelt statements like this about your future employment:

- "It will be in SW Portland."

- "I guess that wine will stay as a hobby, and technology will continue to be my industry."

- "$100K annually is within my reach if I focus on these global employers."

- "The company has to walk its talk about inclusivity and exhibit an accepting environment to LGBTQ employees."

- "The work culture has to support play as well as hard work."

WHAT MATTERS TO YOU?

Before you begin to look for job opportunities, decide what you ideally want, what you will accept, and what is unacceptable to you. This assessment is designed to help you clarify your needs in several categories.

1. **Location.** What is an ideal or acceptable location for your job?
   - **Example 1:** I prefer to work in SW Portland, but would consider up to a 30-minute commute.
   - **Example 2:** I prefer to stay in Portland but would consider large cities on the West Coast, except LA.

2. **Compensation:** What is your goal for compensation? If other factors were right, what would you accept?
   - **Example 1:** My market value is $65K plus good benefits. However, I would accept $55K for an ideal job in a fun work environment. The quality of the medical benefits would affect my decision.
   - **Example 2:** The company needs to match my current base of $100K, plus commission or bonuses.

3. **Industry:** Do you have one or more industries in which you have expertise? If so, which industry, or subset of an industry, would be ideal, acceptable, or unacceptable?
   - **Example 1:** I am a nurse but will no longer work in a hospital. Community health is my ideal, perhaps in a clinic.
   - **Example 2:** I am a controller and my skills could apply to any industry. I prefer education or nonprofits.

4. **Schedule:** What hours do you want to work?
   - **Example 1:** Ideally, I'd like to work the day shift, but am open to swing shift. No night shifts.
   - **Example 2:** I don't want to work more than 40 hours per week (rarely in a pinch) and no on-call.

5. **Culture:** What type of overall work environment and professional values and behaviors are a fit for you?
   - **Example 1:** It is imperative that I have a boss who is inclusive, collaborative, and respectful.
   - **Example 2:** I prefer a relaxed and casual work environment in a thriving and growing company that values their employees' contributions and hard work. I'd accept less than ideal for a short commute.

6. Are there other employer traits that are important to you?
   - **Example 1:** My employer needs to be family-friendly and flexible, allowing for remote work when my kid is sick and the ability to occasionally leave early so I can coach my kid's soccer team.
   - **Example 2:** The company needs to provide training opportunities, so I can advance in my career.

In today's environment, the way we work varies. Some of us work in traditional jobs and receive a salary and benefits from our employers. This allows employers to determine a huge range of variables—from the time you arrive on the job, to whether you can take time off to attend your niece's wedding. In exchange, you receive a dependable paycheck and have clear rights to holidays and vacation.

As you embark on your job search, you may discover that traditional employment is not for you. Instead, you may want more freedom of how, when, and where you work so that you can take as much time off for your niece's wedding as you can finagle into your budget and schedule. By becoming self-employed, you also get to determine your own priorities each day. Your own priorities rule!

There are several models of self-employment to consider:

- **Small Business:** You are an owner in either a brick-and-mortar location or in the world of e-commerce. You may have an entrepreneurial dream to grow this business and hire employees.

- **Contract Employee:** You perform work offered by the employer for a limited time or on a project basis, without perks such as health benefits and paid holidays. For example, you might work at Nike on a one-year contract performing job functions like Nike's full-time exempt employees. At the end of the year, your contract may be renewed or you can contract with another company.

This is considered self-employment because you don't have a long-term commitment to an employer and can simultaneously work for different companies. You can find this type of work either on your own, or through a staffing agency who will issue your paycheck and often offer benefits at your cost.

Note: When you work for a staffing agency, for the duration of your contract you are considered an employee of their agency. Unless otherwise stipulated in your contract with the agency, you generally have only one assignment at a time.

- **Freelancer or Solopreneur:** This is a form of self-employment in which you attract your own clients. Most creative careers (photography, graphic design, copywriting, social media engagement) launch as freelance. Similarly, many therapists and healing professionals work as freelancers/solopreneurs. Being a freelancer requires both entrepreneurial traits as well as a strong web presence.

SELF-EMPLOYMENT ASSESSMENT

If you are thinking about self-employment, take the following assessment to see if you have what it takes to be your own boss. Consider these characteristics and rank each as follows:

3—Very Much Like Me
2—Sometimes Like Me
1—Unlike Me

CHARACTERISTIC	RANK
I do not like to take directions from others.	
After reasonable research, I enjoy a good risk.	
I love a new challenge.	
I rebound from failures quickly.	
Steve Jobs, Mark Zuckerberg, and Jeff Bezos fascinate me, even though they may be irritating.	
I embrace discipline, dedication, and hard work.	
My passion is deep and can be contagious.	
I'm adept at managing money.	
I continually analyze how my bosses could do things better.	
I set goals and persist until they're accomplished.	
TOTAL	

Scoring:
25-33: Give strong consideration to self-employment.
18-24: Consider either self- or traditional employment.
17 and less: Stick with a dependable paycheck.

Before you get started using LinkedIn to research jobs, you might want to skip ahead to the LinkedIn articles in **Step 4: Find Your Networking Style** *to learn how to put together an effective profile and build a basic network that you can call upon for help and information.*

Most people consider LinkedIn to be an online networking tool, but it is more than that. LinkedIn can be incredibly useful for researching job titles held by people who have similar skills and perform the same job functions as you. By viewing company pages on LinkedIn, you can learn more about the companies who have hired people like you (we address this feature in detail in the following article, *Identify Target Employers)*.

VIEW INDIVIDUAL PROFILES TO RESEARCH JOBS

Profiles of LinkedIn members show you how they got started in their careers; you can view their education and entry-level jobs. Plus, if their profile is well-developed, you can learn about the duties and responsibilities of their more advanced jobs to determine if that type of job is a fit for you.

For example, suppose you're looking for a job in the sports marketing industry. Go to the Home page and type "marketing AND sports" in the **Search** field. Then click **People** to get a list of people who have the words *sports and marketing* anywhere in their profile. You could make a chart of 6–12 of those people with their top skills. This will give you an idea if your current background provides a strong enough launching pad to pursue similar positions. You can then search on their job titles to find job postings in LinkedIn as well as Indeed. For more information about using job boards, including LinkedIn, to find position announcements, see *Best Job Boards*.

IDENTIFY PEOPLE FOR INFORMATIONAL INTERVIEWS

The people you find are a good pool of contacts for potential informational interviews. These folks should be local so that you can easily meet up with them. The stated purpose of these interviews is to request the inside scoop on questions like:

- What is the company culture like at X?

- It appears that most employees at X are in their 30s. Is it still a good target company for me given that I am in my 50s?

- Can you tell me something about the hiring process at X?

- Do you know someone else I can meet with who has Y job title in this or similar companies?

In *LinkedIn: Expand and Tap Your Network* we will show you how to get introduced to the folks you identify through connections you have in common ("2nd-degree connections" in LinkedIn lingo). Also, we will show you how to make a request for an informational interview based on a shared interest.

IDENTIFY TARGET EMPLOYERS

Knowing where you want to work might be just as important to you as knowing what type of job you want. Companies have values and personalities, a lot like people. Some are loud and gregarious; some are serious and sophisticated; others are motivated by social good. There are also companies who are perpetually grumpy and hostile—places where you wouldn't want to spend your precious days.

REVIEW WHAT MATTERS TO YOU

Earlier in this section, we asked you to consider what matters to you in a job. We encourage you to revisit what is most important to you, and then identify and research 10–15 employers that could be a potential match. For example:

- If **work/life balance and family** is a priority, you'll want answers to these questions:
  - Is the commute acceptable? If not, is it possible to work remotely?
  - What are typical work weeks? How much vacation time is allotted?
  - What policies do they have for family leave?

- If **security and financial stability** are key for you, you'll want to know:
  - Is the organization growing or changing directions? About to be purchased?
  - What is the organization's source of funding? Is it stable?
  - Does the organization have a reputation for fair compensation?
  - Will there be advancement opportunities?

- If **sustainable and socially responsible practices** are motivators for you, you'll want to know:
  - Do their products or services match your values?
  - Is their workforce and leadership diverse?
  - Do they "walk their talk" around inclusiveness practices?

- Are their sustainability practices congruent with their claims?
- What do they contribute to the community?

TOOLS TO RESEARCH ORGANIZATIONS

Janet Brumbaugh, senior and executive job search coach, spent twenty years as a recruiter. Janet's advice, "If this is a job you really want, get serious, roll up your sleeves and prepare! Because the economy is improving, you may think every company is eager to hire you. Uh-uh! Make no mistake about it; competition is stiff for good, well-paying jobs. Employers EXPECT candidates to be prepared." This means learning about the ins and outs of the company through LinkedIn, Glassdoor, and Google searches.

LINKEDIN

LinkedIn not only features individual profiles, it also allows organizations and businesses to have **company pages**. These pages contain a goldmine of information on company size, recent hires, and the backgrounds of employees holding different positions. You'll also see company news and many position announcements on these pages.

Let's say you are researching clothing companies who have corporate headquarters in Portland. You're curious about Hanna Andertsson, Pendleton Woolen Mills, and Columbia Sportswear. When you go to the employer company pages, you learn the following:

Hanna Andersson has remained stable over the past year with 459 employees. Compare this to Columbia Sportswear, a company that enjoyed a 1 percent annual growth to include 6,901 employees. You'll also note that of the three companies, employees tend to stay longest at Columbia, averaging 5.6 years.

Going further, you'll see a breakdown of employees by Marketing, Sales, Operations, and IT. If you discover the company hires people in your field,

---

Tip

In addition to answering your questions about your target employers, the research you do now will help you shine when you interview with them later.

a next step is to build relationships within the company to answer questions that are not evident on the company page. Learn who in your network is connected to employees in the company and ask for introductions, possible networking meetings, and/or ask your connection to put in a word with the hiring manager when you apply.

See *LinkedIn for Job Research* for other ways in which you can use this valuable tool to identify target employers.

GLASSDOOR.COM

This site provides employee reviews and insider information for 600,000 companies. Ratings are posted by past and current employees. In our example, on January 1, 2018, you would see:

- Hannah Anderson has 94 reviews and an average rating of 3.0 out of five.

- Pendleton Woolen Mills has 48 reviews and an average rating of 2.9 out of five.

- Columbia Sportswear has 384 reviews and stands out with an average rating 3.4 out of five.

You might conclude that quite a few disgruntled employees wrote reviews and there isn't that much difference. However, if you look a little deeper you would see some trends emerge. In response to "Would you recommend the employer to a friend?" Columbia stands out with a 69 percent "yes" rating. Also, locally grown Tim Boyle is the favored CEO with an 89 percent approval rating. Your decision to focus on Columbia is further bolstered by graphs of growth on the stock market.

You could then dive deeper into the comments to get more details about the culture, management style, and practices that informed those reviews.

COMPANY WEBSITE AND GOOGLE

Some of Janet Brumbaugh's tips for employer research include:

- Read their website. Don't just glance, devour it! What's the latest? What foundations or charities do they support? Any recent mergers or acquisitions? What terms are germane to their product and industry? Are there links to news articles about outstanding accomplishments?

- Web resources like LinkedIn, Glassdoor, and Google often will reveal the company's history, finances, competitors, and challenges. Pay attention to what's hot and how the company is positioned to meet trends. While the company's website will have links to positive press, scout out newspaper articles that spotlight some challenges that they are facing.

CONTACT YOUR NETWORK

LinkedIn company pages show your 1st- and 2nd-degree connections who work or have worked for the organization. See which groups and professional associations they belong to so you can engage with them, either in LinkedIn groups or at face-to-face events they attend. If you know a connection well, you might want to invite them to tea to discuss more frankly the insider's view of the company's strengths and blemishes. If you want to build relationships with 2nd-degree connections, see *LinkedIn: Expand and Tap Your Network*.

Step 2
Find Position Openings—
Who Wants You?

"Be open to the amazing changes which are occurring in the field that interests you."
—Leigh Steinberg

You now have a clearer vision of your job destination. If you are a visual person, you might even enjoy imagining the pleasant commute, smiling coworkers, a boss asking for your opinion and other traits you value. You might want to visualize an empty desk and the team searching for someone exactly like you.

Finding job openings that match what you want is full of uncertainty. You may wonder:

- "Do my skills and experience match those in job postings?"
- "Does the job I want in one of my target companies actually exist?"
- "How can I begin to decipher the code with keywords, filters, and job boards?"

In this section we'll help you answer those questions; we'll explain how to find open positions that match your qualifications and criteria for the job you want.

In *Find Jobs on the Internet* we give you tips for scanning job postings, help you determine which jobs to apply for, and when you can ignore the "rules" of when or when not to apply.

There are many online sources for job postings and in *Best Job Boards* we help you sort through them. We offer practical tips for using the most common job boards such as Indeed and LinkedIn as well as several government and industry-specific job boards.

Social media platforms are also a good source of position announcements. In *Facebook for Job Search* and *Twitter for Job Search* we offer tips on incorporating these enormously popular social media sites into your job search strategy.

Not all work arrangements are "traditional," meaning you are hired by a company as a salaried employee who goes to work at the same office every day. In fact, there is an increasing trend towards remote, freelance, and temporary employment to accommodate a workforce that is wanting more autonomy and greater work/life balance. In *Remote Employment* and *Contract and Freelance Work* we address these trends and show you how to find full-time remote employment and temporary or freelance work.

Sometimes reaching out to recruiters and hiring managers is the best job search strategy, particularly if jobs in your industry are found primarily through word-of-mouth. *Engage Recruiters and Hiring Managers*, written by our associate, Janet Brumbaugh, describes the different types or recruiters and how to get their attention. It also offers tips for building relationships with hiring managers.

You may find that you need to refine specific skills or enhance industry knowledge to land your ideal job in your target industry or company. In this case, *Internships: Posted or Self-Designed* and *Sample Request for Internship* can help you find an internship to move you toward your ultimate employment goals.

Finally, in *Job Search for the Older Candidate* we help you find employers that are friendly to the "over 50" workforce and offer concrete strategies for job hunting that are specific to the older candidate.

Now, let's find a job posting that's a match for you!

FIND JOBS ON THE INTERNET

Social media, job boards, researching companies, and online networking play a major role in finding jobs. However, with so many job boards, LinkedIn options, social media platforms, and company websites, finding jobs online can make your head spin! In this article and the ones that follow, we help you devise an online job search strategy that will minimize stress while optimizing your time and keeping you sane.

ORGANIZE YOUR SEARCH

How you search depends on your job target and industry. For most people, we recommend a mix of two or three general job boards and one other that is specific to your industry (see the next article *Best Job Boards* for our recommendations). We also recommend you identify 15 to 20 employer sites, and two or three career-specific bulletin boards or websites. If you're a fan of social media, you might want to check out the job listings on your favorite platform (later we explain how to look for jobs on Facebook and Twitter).

Begin with a broad exploration of different sites and job boards to see which platforms you enjoy, and which are the most fruitful. Then, bookmark your favorites and check them on a regular basis. Set aside a fixed day and time—for example, Monday and Thursday evenings—to search for jobs. We want you to sustain your drive and energy, so we recommend limiting your time to no more than 90 minutes, twice a week. However, if you are thirty minutes into reviewing postings and you see a perfect fit, stop reviewing and switch your effort to tailoring a resume and cover letter to that job. We show you how to do this in the next section, *Step 3: Prepare Your Resume and Cover Letter*.

HOW TO SCAN ONLINE POSTINGS

The length of online postings varies; some are only half a page while others go on for two–three pages. Reading longer postings can be arduous, especially if the minimum qualifications for the job come after a lengthy description of the company, job duties, and softer skills.

To avoid a useless time sink, read just a few lines of the duties—enough to know if you are interested. Then, jump straight to the section that describes the "must haves" for the job, usually defined as qualifications and/or requirements. If you don't have at least the top four concrete requirements (years of experience, degrees, and skills), then you are probably not a candidate and you do not need to spend more of your precious time reading the rest of the posting.

Some postings do not say much about the required qualifications. In this case, read the job duties and ask yourself, "Can I demonstrate that I've performed over 75 percent of these duties?" If so, you may be a qualified candidate and it is worth your time to apply.

SHOULD I APPLY?

The first consideration is to determine if you have at least a moderate level of interest. If you are adequately interested, ask yourself if you are competitive for the position: what are your chances of getting an interview in which you can learn more about whether the job meets your true needs? To determine if you have a reasonable chance, further scrutinize the qualifications listed in the position announcement. If you meet at least 75 percent of the qualifications, it is worth it to take the time to tailor your resume. The announcement's wording can give you clues as to the relative importance of the listed qualifications:

Tip

*If you are unemployed, you might have the energy and desire to devote more than 90 minutes to job search. That is just great, but remember to give yourself plenty of breaks and rewards for self-care. If you are employed, you will need to be more strategic and disciplined with your time. It will save you time in the long run to learn how to set filters on sites such as Indeed and LinkedIn. We show you how to do this in **Best Job Boards**.*

DON'T SEND OUT THE SAME RESUME TO EVERY EMPLOYER

Tifini has had clients come to her after sending out a few hundred unrequited resumes. Not surprisingly, this leads to despair. Chances are, you lack some qualifications or haven't highlighted the qualifications you do have pertinent to the job announcement.

Abandon the high-volume, long-shot approach of sending out copies of the same resume to hundreds of employers. Instead, adopt the practice of applying for fewer, better-matched jobs with targeted resumes, while also implementing other tactics outlined in this handbook.

- **Is the qualification "required" or "minimum"?** Assume that the tracking system (for more information see *Applicant Tracking Software* in the next section) is set to assign the highest number of points to the required hard skills. For example, if it requires "five years of project management in an Agile environment," you should only apply if you can prove that on your resume.

- **Is the qualification identified as "preferred" or "desirable"?** Apply if you are missing a skill/experience labeled "preferred" or "desirable" rather than "required."

- **Are the qualifications listed in a short want ad or at the bottom of a longer position announcement?** If an employer is paying for an ad by the word, they probably have chosen the most important elements for the ad. An employer who lists "Experience with Raiser's Edge" in a three-line ad is very serious about this requirement. In contrast, an employer who places the same software in a laundry list of desirable skills at the end of a one-page position announcement is likely to be flexible, even if it is labeled as a "requirement."

WHEN SHOULD I IGNORE THE RULES?

There are several reasons to override our good advice and apply when you don't meet nearly all the high-priority requirements:

1. Consider applying **if you know someone of possible influence inside the organization** who will put in a good word for you. Vicki's daughter, Jessica, combed her network relentlessly until she found someone at Michael Hoff Productions who gave the person sorting resumes a call and said, "Don't overlook that Jessica. She is really great." She got the interview.

2. **If you can take less than an hour to tailor a resume and cover letter** you may want to apply to some long shots. Keep in mind, though, that sinking too much time and pinning your hopes on positions which require qualifications you don't have can leave you feeling unwanted and unloved. Most employers no longer send out rejection letters, so your resume might end up going into the "resume black hole."

3. Consider applying **if you want to work in a rare field that has more openings than applicants or requires a highly specialized skill you possess**. For example, social service jobs that indicate "bilingual in Spanish" or "Russian reading and writing preferred" will have a limited number of applicants. These organizations will look more seriously at candidates missing some other qualification. Similarly, if you work in high tech and your knowledge of PHP or R programming language includes the latest released version, you might be a shoo-in.

If you are still not sure how much job postings are worth your time, give them a test. Actively search for a month and send out resumes. It can't hurt and there is something satisfying about sending in a resume as opposed to networking because you know, without a doubt, that there is an opening.

Tip

You will also want to ignore our emphasis on finding jobs online if you are in a field where positions are very rarely posted. Some positions, such as those in the arts, are usually secured through word of mouth. Spend a few solid evenings experimenting with several keywords on a variety of sites to see if you come up with a hit or a near hit. If you don't get any hits, the bulk of your time will need to be spent networking and getting yourself in front of hiring managers, rather than searching online.

BEST JOB BOARDS

After you've identified possible employers and researched the job titles that interest you, the next step is finding position announcements that match your criteria. This is where the myriad of job boards and aggregate search engines come in handy! We'll tell you about a few that we consider the best and give you some tips on how to use them effectively.

INDEED.COM

This is the best aggregate site for all job postings online. It pulls in jobs from thousands of websites, including job boards, staffing agencies, company job postings, and professional associations. Learning how to use Indeed's advanced features will serve you well in your job search. Here are six tips to get you started:

1. After you get past the basic search screen, click the **Advanced Job Search** link. This is where you set filters to customize your search.

2. Make sure to set the **Salary Estimate** and **Location** options so you get listings of jobs that pay what you want at the companies where you want to work.

3. The **With These Words in the Title** field is where you type in the job titles you've identified. If the title contains two words, then surround it in quotes. For example, "project coordinator."

4. The **With At Least One of These Words** field is often a good place to narrow your search to a specific industry. For example, if you want to find a project coordinator job in the health care industry, type "health care" in this field.

5. The **With None of These Words** field applies to the description of the job. This is where you type in the name of industries in which you don't want to work. For example, if you don't want a job in IT or software, you type "IT, software" here.

6. Use the **Job Alert** feature to have Indeed email you job announcements that meet your full criteria.

LINKEDIN.COM

Not only is LinkedIn a great networking and research tool, but it's an excellent source for finding job announcements. Its job search features and how they integrate with your network are incredibly robust. We'll give you some tips to get you started but recommend that you experiment with LinkedIn's job search feature on your own to get a feel for all it has to offer.

Note: Before using LinkedIn to look for jobs, make sure your LinkedIn profile is in top shape. For more information, see **LinkedIn: Create an Effective Profile**.

To start your LinkedIn job search, click **Jobs** on the toolbar and then type a job title, company name, or other keyword. A drop-down menu of suggested titles and companies appears, making it easy for you to select what you want. Enter your location— Portland, OR, for example—and then pick the area in which you want to search. Several filters appear below the search bar.

Here are six tips for using the filters:

1. The **Date Posted** filter refines your search to only those jobs posted within a certain time frame. This makes it easy to view the most recently posted jobs.

2. Use the **Company** filter to see which companies have jobs that match your selected job title.

Tip

Over time, working remotely has become increasingly popular; many companies now offer jobs that can be done away from the office. The way you find these jobs depends on the job board. For example, to find remote jobs on Indeed, type "Remote" in the **Location** *field. Most other job boards have "remote," "telecommute," or "home-based working" as one of their Location filters. For a list of job boards that cater specifically to virtual workers, see* **Remote Employment and Contract and Freelance Work**.

When you begin, explore different keywords and job titles to see which yield the best matches. Does the word green *pull up more jobs about golf courses or sustainability? Does the phrase* communication coordinator *tend to pull up jobs that require numerous software programs?*

You can use complex phrases to refine your search. Most job boards recognize AND, OR, and NOT (known as Boolean logic) in the **title field**. *For example, suppose you want to search for a project coordinator position on Indeed, but you know you aren't interested in technical positions in software companies. In the* **With These Words in the Title** *field you would type: "project coordinator" NOT (technical OR software). Notice the use of parentheses here. Don't forget the quotes! Most job boards require them for job titles with two or more words.*

3. The **Experience Level** feature helps you limit your search to only those jobs that match your level.

4. The **All Filters** option is handy for finding postings in a particular industry or field. For example, you could find all the project coordinator jobs in project management within the computer software industry. You can add as many industries as you like. For example, you can type "financial services" in the box above the list to see if there are project coordinator jobs in that industry. If you're a creative type, you might type in "fine arts" or "entertainment" to find project coordinator jobs in those industries.

5. Once you've set your filters for the selected job title or company, you can click **Create Search Alert** to receive LinkedIn notifications when job announcements matching your criteria are posted.

6. If you want to apply for a job, use the **LinkedIn Features** filter to find jobs that have less than 10 applicants and which ones are **Easy Apply** jobs. Choosing postings with minimal applicants can increase your chances of getting an interview IF you meet the job requirements.

GOOGLE JOBS

Google jobs is a powerful tool for finding jobs posted across the web—from small company websites to large job boards posting thousands of listings. Before using Google Jobs, experiment with Indeed and LinkedIn to find out which keywords or job titles yield

results. Then, plug those same keywords or titles into Google Jobs to get a more comprehensive list of position announcements. Here's how:

1. Make sure you have Google Chrome installed.

2. In the Google search bar, type the job title or keyword in quotes followed by "jobs." For example, if you're looking for program manager positions, you would type "program manager" followed by the word *jobs*. Google automatically knows your location, so you'll see a list of postings in your area.

3. The **Title, Location, Date Posted, Type, Company Type,** and **Employer** filters make it easy to refine your search according to the factors you desire in a job.

4. Use **Company Type** to search for jobs in a particular industry. In our example, you can find program manager jobs in the health care industry by selecting **Health Care** under **Company Type**.

5. Click on a job listing to see more information about the job, shown to the right of your screen. Google Jobs provides a wealth of information about each position announcement beyond just the job description. You can find out on which job board the position was originally posted (and then go there to apply), typical salary ranges, and links to company reviews and more job postings at the company.

MACSLIST.ORG

Mac's List was created by Portlander Mac Prichard to help local job seekers find quality jobs, internships, and volunteer opportunities in the Portland area. It includes keyword search capabilities and is well worth a look if you're interested in communications, education, nonprofit, government, health care, and technology jobs as well as internships or volunteer opportunities.

In addition to postings, Mac's List offers quality podcasts and an excellent blog about job searching in Portland. Mac's List's calendar of events is a great place to learn about classes, seminars, and local networking opportunities.

GOVERNMENT JOB BOARDS

- **USAJOBS.gov:** This board lists a variety of government jobs anywhere in the country and is incredibly easy to use with self-explanatory keywords, location fields, and robust filters. Here are four tips for using the filters:

1. The **Hiring Path** filter shows you how many federal jobs containing the keywords you entered are open to the general public, federal employees, employees within an agency, recent graduates, etc. Hovering over each hiring path gives you specifics about who can apply.

2. Use the **Pay** filter to search for jobs that match a certain salary range or GS scale. GS scales have different education requirements. You'll want to research the various GS scales to see if you qualify. This website is an excellent place to start your research: **http://govcentral. monster.com/benefits/articles/1757-what-determines-where-you-stand-on-the-gs-scale**

3. Explore the **Department & Agency** and **Series** filters to see which departments and agencies have jobs matching your keywords, and the titles of the positions posted.

4. Explore the **More Filters** tab to narrow your search.

- **GovernmentJobs.com** is another easy-to-use national government job board. From the home page, search by job title (Category) or city (Location). The filters to the left allow you to refine your search based on distance, date posted, government organization, category, and salary requirements.

- **Oregon.gov/EMPLOY/jobseekers/Pages/ Government-Jobs.aspx** is where you can search for government jobs in Oregon by county, city, and state. For further job-seeking assistance or if you are looking for private-sector jobs, the Oregon.gov/ EMPLOY site is another excellent resource.

OTHER JOB BOARDS WORTH EXPLORING

- **Idealist.org:** a national job board for jobs in nonprofit and sustainability.

- **Poachedjobs.com:** jobs in the food and beverage industry.

- **Dice.com:** a national job board for technical jobs. Includes great articles about working in the tech industry and the skills needed as well as a career exploration and salary research feature.

- **Portlandtech.org:** a local job board that lists technical jobs in the greater Portland and Vancouver areas. This board is extra handy because you can search by specific development environments (mobile dev, web dev, network/ systems), languages (java, Ruby, PHP, C#, etc.), design/UI/UX, and other supportive roles (business analyst, sales, customer service, etc.). In addition, this is a great job board for finding internships and entry-level technical jobs.

- **Flexjobs.com:** a great resource for remote, part-time, and freelance work. We go into more detail about this job board in the *Remote Employment* article.

Tip

*Need help understanding how to use the USAJOBS filters? The help system for this site is extremely helpful—easy to access and well-written. Just click the **Help** link next to each filter.*

- **Craigslist.com:** a good site for part-time jobs and one-time "gigs." Many creative and out-of-the-box jobs are posted here.

  Note: Use craigslist with caution! It attracts scammers and listings that do not name the employer. If something about a craigslist posting just doesn't "feel right," listen to your instinct and avoid it.

- **Careerbuilder.com:** a popular job board but with fewer advanced search features than Indeed and fewer filters than LinkedIn or Google Jobs. You have to sign up for full access to all its features.

- **Simplyhired.com:** another aggregator site that is gaining popularity.

- **Glassdoor.com:** a job board plus a great resource for company reviews and researching company interview practices, work environment, and salaries. You do, however, need a subscription to access all its features.

- **Job boards from professional associations**, such as WVDO (Willamette Valley Development Officers) or PRSA (Public Relations Association of America).

Note: We've provided a few procedures on how to use certain features on Indeed, LinkedIn, and government job boards. Keep in mind the user experience on job boards often changes. While Indeed has stayed fairly consistent over time, LinkedIn changes more frequently. Your best bet is to use the board's help feature (if they have one) or search the internet for "how to…" articles.

WHAT IF I'M NOT FINDING VERY MANY JOBS?

If you find that your search is not bearing much fruit, there are a few tricks you can try:

1. Scan the position titles and descriptions for new keywords to try.

2. Reduce the salary and expand the geographical range to see if that produces more results.

3. Experiment with the same keywords in Seattle, even if you don't want to move. The Seattle market is twice as big as Portland's and you can check if your keywords are accurate.

WHAT TO DO WITH YOUR RESULTS

You may come across several jobs that sound perfect and maybe they are! To figure out if you are likely to compete for the job, you must either meet at least the top four skills and experience requirements for the job or know someone inside the organization who can put in a good word for you. For more information to determine if you should apply, see *Find Jobs on the Internet.*

Also, it's best to apply only for jobs that have been posted in the last two weeks or have a closing date for submitting applications. If you meet the requirements and decide to apply, you will need to tailor your resume to show that you have the skills and background to do the job. We show you how in the *Prepare Your Resume and Cover Letter* section of this book.

LEARN FROM THE RESULTS

Searching for jobs will teach you a lot about the job market and the skills that are in demand in your field or industry. Pay attention to these three factors to learn more and make yourself more marketable:

1. Notice if there are technical skills coming up frequently that you could learn relatively quickly to make yourself more competitive.

2. **Develop a networking strategy** if you are in a field with few job postings. Remember, only 30 percent of people get jobs without using a networking strategy. We show you how to develop a network in *Step 4, Find Your Networking Style.*

3. **Identify organizations to follow** and research their websites to find out about problems they are trying to solve and who they hire to solve them. Follow them on LinkedIn and see if you can make new connections with people who work there.

Finally, stay persistent and stay connected. When your energy sags, take an afternoon off and reward yourself for your hard efforts by trying one of our *gifts to give yourself.*

FACEBOOK FOR JOB SEARCH

Facebook is the largest social networking site, with over 2.2 billion active members. It is also the most visited; more than 70 percent of Facebook users are on the site every day.

Although it is primarily considered a social site, a growing number of recruiters are joining Facebook to post job announcements and research prospective candidates. While LinkedIn still leads the pack—used by 87 percent of recruiters—a healthy 55 percent have reported using Facebook. With a statistic like that it isn't surprising that Facebook is becoming more relevant as a job search tool.

IS SEARCHING FOR JOBS ON FACEBOOK FOR YOU?

If you are against Facebook's policies and practices, then by all means, do not incorporate it as part of your job search strategy. That being said, it can be a useful tool. We recommend you seriously consider using Facebook as part of your job search if:

- **You have a large network of friends and family members on Facebook**. You can publicize your talents and job search intentions to your network and ask members to introduce you to people they know. Not only could these introductions expand your list of "Friends," but they could be a source for job leads.

- **The employers you are targeting have Facebook pages**. You can "Like" an employer's page, engage with them, and research their company by following links on their page to their websites and blogs. In addition, company Facebook pages may contain information about benefits, culture, and hiring practices, as well as post jobs and accept applications.

- **You are seeking positions that desire expertise in social media**. Showing you are active on Facebook, both as a casual user and as a professional, demonstrates your savvy social media skills.

- **You are gainfully employed and have a lifestyle or political side business**. For example, you might have a day job as a technical writer, but also have a side gig writing political articles and blog posts that generate a small income stream. You might want to have your straight-day-job-identity on LinkedIn and your side business on Facebook, which has a more personal, human emphasis.

TIPS FOR JOB SEARCH ON FACEBOOK

Here are three tips to maximize Facebook's job search potential:

1. **Tap your network of Friends:** Keep in mind it's very difficult to get through HR screening unless your skills exactly meet the key qualifications listed in a job announcement. Without an exact match, you are dependent on your connections to put in a good word for you to get your resume in the hands of the hiring manager. If the people who care about your success are your Facebook friends, we recommend that you tap them for connections to your desired employers when you are applying for a job.

2. **Join Facebook groups:** There are many groups, small and large, for job seekers interested in specific fields. The Social Media and Marketing Jobs Facebook group, for example, is a larger group with around 54,000 members! Check out groups in Business and Organizations and join a few that you think are the most appealing and may be the most helpful. Don't dismiss groups that are small or local. They may have higher engagement, a deeper focus, and more local connections than large groups.

3. **Use the Search feature to find job listings:** Type "Portland Oregon jobs" in the search bar and you will find a few hundred listings. You can then narrow down the list by checking the industry you are interested in.

These additional Facebook job search features are recommended by Hannah Morgan of **Job-Hunt.org.** Check out her site at **job-hunt.org/social-networking/ facebook-job-search.shtml**.

1. **Check your privacy settings:** Facebook has a reputation for changing privacy setting criteria, so it is a good idea to review yours often. To ensure your privacy, click on the down arrow at the top right of your screen. Click on **Settings**, and then click on **Privacy** (there is a lock next to the command). You'll see several privacy options you can edit. Make sure you have selected the best ones for your situation.

2. **Edit your profile:** You don't have to become a regular Facebook user to create a well-crafted profile that emphasizes your skills, education, and experience. Many of the same guidelines for creating your LinkedIn profile apply to creating your Facebook profile as well. For example, it is important to add past work history and professional skills to your About section.

   Keep in mind that you'll need to delete material that you would not want a prospective employer to see. Also, it's against Facebook's Terms of Use to set up a separate professional profile. Instead, learn how to adjust your settings and monitor your account more closely to be quirky and social with personal friends, and less so with professional networks.

3. **Use Facebook Lists:** You can select who you want to see your status updates. Think of it as an email distribution list. You may decide to set up separate lists for your close friends, personal interests, and your professional contacts. Your lists might look like this:
   - **"Personal friends"** are friends you're more likely to share personal information with.
   - **"Custom: Sustainable Food"** might be folks who share your professional interest in the organic food industry. For example, you could share your posts about the latest trends in organic farming and food policies to this list to build your credibility and expertise in this field.
   - **"Custom: Spirituality"**: posting to this list would allow you to share resources and leads relevant to your faith, without negatively impacting your job search.

Facebook is not only a fun and informative site to keep in touch with friends and family, but also a powerful tool for researching potential employers, building professional contacts, and finding job openings. We think it is a site with vast job search potential that should not be overlooked! If you haven't done so yet, take the plunge into Facebook and see what jobs you can find.

TWITTER FOR JOB SEARCH

Twitter is a microblogging service in which you can follow the messages of other people, organizations, and companies and they can follow yours. A message, limited to 140 characters, is referred to as a "tweet." You will see the tweets of anyone you follow and whoever follows you will see your tweets. These shared messages can create a vast network of beneficial connections.

Twitter is one of many social media applications job seekers can use to brand themselves, network in their desired industry, and conduct a widespread job search. Also, actively tweeting can gain the attention of employers and recruiters. If you are using other applications such as LinkedIn and Facebook for job search, you may want to consider adding Twitter. Connecting Twitter to LinkedIn makes sharing articles and comments easier and expands your social media toolkit.

A little different from other social media applications, Twitter's platform is unique because it allows for multiple accounts; you can have your personal Twitter account focused on hobbies and interests, and a separate professional account to brand you and focus on specific industries and employers.

TWITTER JOB SEARCH TIPS

Here are seven recommendations to successfully use this job search tool:

1. Be consistent with your online branding. Use the same profile photo and tagline for Twitter as you do for your LinkedIn and Facebook accounts.

2. Start networking by following industry leaders, organizations, publications, recruiters, and job forums. Join conversations, retweet, and reply to tweets in meaningful ways that make you stand out.

3. Keep an eye out for job postings in your Twitter feed; some companies only post their position announcements on social media.

4. Monitor your industry for recent business developments—this can give you an indication of a potential round of hiring and create good small-talk topics.

5. Research potential employers. If you have an upcoming interview, research the hiring manager. Their tweets could clue you into topics of interest.

6. Type "Portland jobs" in the search field. A list will appear of jobs in Portland in different sectors. Pick the sector that interests you and looks through the tweets. Not only will you find out who is hiring in general, but you'll find specific job openings and announcements for networking events and job fairs.

7. Experiment with #hashtags. Try typing in different #hashtag combinations and see what pops up in the list. For example, if you type #techjobs, you can get an idea of who is tweeting what about jobs in the tech industry. You can also get a sense of what related hashtags those sites reference. For example, many sites using the #tech hashtag, also use the #science hashtag.

Above all, remember that what you put out on Twitter is visible to a massive audience so only post what you'd feel comfortable sharing with a potential employer. Keep your tweets, retweets, and comments focused on promoting what you have to offer future employers and staying up-to-date in your industry. Happy tweeting!

NO CUBES FOR MIRIAM

When Vicki's younger daughter Miriam was a teenager, she assured Vicki that she would never work from 9 to 5 in a cube. At the time, Vicki assumed Miriam would eventually learn the hard fact: most careers demand that structured office time with two weeks of vacation time.

In college, Miriam studied abroad in Florence, Italy, where she quickly felt at home. She vowed to return.

Miriam currently works remotely as a translator from Italian to English. Sitting by a window looking down on a piazza, her work runs the gamut from tourism blogs to anthropology dissertations. When Miriam became a single mother, working remotely on her own schedule made it easier to perform the always complicated work/parenting balancing act.

A side benefit for Vicki is that she has a beautiful place to visit to enjoy amazing food, art, and the Mediterranean climate of Italy.

Do you want to work at home, in your favorite coffee shop, or on a beach in Bali? When we wrote the previous version of this handbook in 2012 the only way to do so was to work as a contractor or start a business. In other words, to work remotely you had to forgo the perks of traditional employment: medical benefits, retirement, paid time off, and greater job security.

Fortunately, a new trend is on the rise—many employers are now adopting what is called a distributed workforce. This means that employees do not work at one central brick-and-mortar location. Instead, they perform their work entirely on the phone, by email, or through teleconferencing. Yes—even from that beach in Bali! Some jobs are partially remote, which would limit you to those within geographical reach—living in Bali would have to wait, but you could still take a working vacation there.

Note: When remote work was first introduced, it was called telecommuting. You may still come across this term today, but it means the same thing as remote work.

WHY IS REMOTE WORK A VIABLE TREND?

Just a few years ago, employers were hesitant about remote employment; they were concerned that unsupervised employees would not be as productive as their counterparts in the office. Research has now shown the opposite to be true: remote workers tend to work longer hours with strong productivity.

Another reason for this trend is that the strong economy has made it challenging for many employers to attract local talent for specialized positions. As a result, the types of positions open for remote work have moved far beyond the early days when they were almost exclusively tech jobs. Business Insider predicts that 50 percent of the workforce will work remotely (at least part of the time) by 2020.

SAMPLE REMOTE JOB TITLES

A scan of the 42 categories of jobs on Virtual Vocations yields this enormous range:

- Writer on the topic of acupuncture and oriental medicine

- Virtual Nursing Faculty member to teach online

- Senior Solution Sales Engineer

- Social Media Manager

- Sales Representative for an apparel company

HOW TO FIND REMOTE EMPLOYMENT

You can find remote employment in three ways:

1. Explore the general sites listed below.

2. Drill down to industry-specific sites. For example, **www.toptal.com** is for finance experts and software engineers and designers.

3. Google "100 percent remote companies" and you will see a list of companies that hire all remote workers as well as articles that describe them.

RECOMMENDED JOB BOARDS FOR REMOTE EMPLOYMENT

When we googled "Best Remote Job Boards," we were led to this article: **breathingtravel.com/best-sites-to-your-dream-remote-job**. It lists the 20 best job boards for finding remote work. We discovered that many are by subscription, with access to limited features for free. If you are serious about finding remote employment, it may be worth your time to explore all the job boards in the Breathing Travel article, and then make the investment in one of more of your favorites. Here are a few of ours:

- **Indeed.com** is our go-to job board because it is free and has excellent keyword filters. In the Location field, you can type "remote." For more information on using Indeed, see *Best Job Boards* earlier in this handbook.

- **FlexJobs.com** lists remote, freelance, and flexible employment. The FlexJobs team reviews and researches each posting to make sure it is a legitimate part- or full-time opportunity. There is a small fee for a one-month trial, but it is worth it to circumvent hours of chasing false ads. You can look at the list of posted jobs for free, but you cannot see the full posting until you register and pay the fee.

- **Jobspresso.com** is constantly updated and expertly curated to include only legitimate, open, and recent

job posts. The user experience is superb with filters and search fields easy to find and use.

- **VirtualVocations.com** offers over 10,000 telecommuting (the term they use) jobs, including business services, tech, travel, education, and accounting positions, administrative support, and nonprofit jobs. This easy-to-use job board is one of our favorites because of its robust filters—you can find jobs that are at any level (from internships to executive) with the amount of telecommuting you want: 100 percent, Majority, Frequently, or Occasionally. These examples only scratch the surface of the filters offered by Virtual Vocations, to help you find the jobs that match your criteria.

COMPANIES WITH 100 PERCENT REMOTE EMPLOYEES

We googled "Employers with 100% Remote Employees" and then came up with a list of several companies that are completely remote. Here is a sampling, which are broadly in the technology arena.

- **10up** provides web design and development consulting services. They describe their 120+ person team as «one big happy family"—a family that's distributed worldwide and stays connected via Slack, Google Hangout, and plain old texting.

- **Automattic** is the remote team that is the genius behind WordPress, Longreads, Simplenote, Gravatar, and Polldaddy, and other tools many rely on day in, day out for their business needs. «Automatticians» work from anywhere they want; their current team of nearly 500 employees is located in over 50 countries.

- **Fire Engine RED** provides marketing, technology, and data solutions to the education market with over 80 employees across North America.

Tip

*If you're interested in working for a company that is 100 percent remote or offers mostly remote employment with a small headquartered office, check out the blog on **Zapier.com** for a list of options: **zapier.com/blog/companies-hiring-remote-workers**.*

A full-time, long-term job in which you travel to the employer's location may not mesh with your needs. Do one or more of these characteristics describe you?

- Working this much, plus a commute, isn't congruent with my values or lifestyle—I crave time and flexibility for passion-driven pursuits like music, gardening, or activism.

- I'm a parent with young children and my family needs trump the needs of an employer.

- I have physical or emotional conditions not compatible with the demands of a full-time commitment.

- I live far from the city or have an untenable commute to traditional workplaces on a traditional schedule.

- I'm in a field (such as photography or cartooning) where there is a lack of traditional employment.

- I want to live and/or travel to Thailand or other exotic and affordable destinations.

You aren't alone—the freelance and contract segments of a changing workforce that wants more flexibility have been the fastest growing aspects of the job market. Just look around at your corner coffee shop and you'll see folks on their laptops, sipping a latte while they work.

WHAT IS A CONTRACT JOB?

A contract jobs is paid work for which you are hired for a limited time or to complete a specific project. Such workers are called independent contractors who either find their own contracts or go through a staffing agency who finds work for them. Contractors do not receive traditional benefits such as health care, paid time off, or retirement. Sometimes the pay is excellent to compensate for the lack of benefits; sometimes the pay is crummy.

Note: Some staffing agencies do offer health benefits. Although they have negotiated lower rates with the insurance company, the contractor must pay 100 percent of the cost of the benefits they want.

Economists predict that contracted work arrangements will become more frequent than traditional employment. This trend is driven partly by people who don't fit into a traditional work box and by millennials who want more work/life balance. There is, however, a great deal of controversy over employers with many contract workers. Companies claim contract workers are required to meet ever changing business demands—they claim they need flexibility to hire and let go of workers quickly and easily. Opponents claim it is a way for companies to avoid paying benefits and provide job stability to their workers.

SAMPLE CONTRACT JOBS

As you can see from the examples below, contract jobs vary wildly. They may require basic or specialized advanced skills, be as short as a few days (sometimes called a *gig*), or be as long as several years. The pay may be excellent for high-demand professionals such as software developers and engineers. In the cases below, the workers didn't have to market their own services; customers were provided by a company or the worker was placed on assignment by a staffing firm.

- *Denaya* drives for Lyft during the hours her kids are in school.

- *Gwenn* has been an environmental compliance specialist for BPA for four years. Two-thirds of her team are contractors hired through staffing agencies, rather than full-time employees.

- *Dimitri* is an in-home caregiver for seniors, placed by Caregiver Connection, a referral company.

- *Vicki* was on contract for an internship advisor at PCC, filling in for a three-month maternity leave.

- *Sabrina* is an on-call social worker in Portland half of the year, spending the other half in Costa Rica.

- Most of *Leslie's* technical writing career at Microsoft was spent as an independent contractor or as a temporary employee working through a staffing agency. She moved from project to project in different departments every 6–12 months.

ADVANTAGES OF CONTRACT WORK
There are many:

- **You can take an employer for a test run**. Filling a time-limited contract can be an effective way to find out if you like the job duties, culture, and your teammates. It gives you a doorway out if you aren't happy as well as a possible doorway in—but don't count on that door being open, even if you prove your merit. If traditional full-time employment is your goal, you'll want to know ahead of time if the company typically converts contractors to full-time employees.

- **You get to take time off between jobs**. By law contracts are time-limited, so you can plan for breaks between jobs to devote to family, study, or creative projects.

  One of our clients worked on contract with Nike as a photographer for six years. Nike offered him ten months on the job with a two-month break each year. He used the break to pursue his own nature photography. He even enjoyed the perk of receiving unemployment because technically, he was laid off.

- **You might be able to enjoy more flexibility**. Many, but not all, contracting arrangements allow more autonomy on how, where, and when you carry out your job duties.

- **More direct compensation** may be provided in lieu of benefits. If you're receiving benefits through another source (maybe through your partner's job), you may enjoy having more cash at your digression.

DISADVANTAGES OF CONTRACT WORK
There is a flip side to the advantages of this looser, short-term work arrangement:

- **No retirement perks**. If you are traditionally employed with the government or a company that has a retirement plan, these accumulate without any effort on your part. When you are a contractor/freelancer, it's up to you to set aside money for retirement. This can be very challenging if you are on a tight budget.

- **Commitment** is low for the employer. If they don't like the color of your new tattoo, they can give you notice without a cause. You have no performance reviews or performance improvement plans to address weaknesses.

- **Team comradery** is often lacking because your colleagues know you are a short-timer and may believe that you're not as committed to the company as they are.

WHO ARE FREELANCERS?
Freelancers are mostly folks who work for themselves in creative fields, such as photography, web development, copywriting, and design. Freelancers are often simultaneously contractors with more than one client at a time.

There are three ways creative freelancers generate income. They may use one or all these methods as their needs change:

1. Develop a web presence and market their services to attract their own customers who pay directly. Most freelancers write simple contracting agreements with their clients. Senior-level creatives often have contracts on a retainer (guaranteed number of hours) with their favorite clients.

2. Work through a creative staffing agency, like a contractor, to be placed in a company on a

*Sean Yates, our book designer, has a common story shared by many creatives—his work history is a potpourri of different work arrangements. While in the Washington, DC area, he held a solid position as an illustrator/designer for a global company doing DVD covers for giants like RLJ Entertainment and MHz Networks. When he left the DC area in 2015, he launched his website and gained several small clients as a freelancer. When his savings began to diminish, he took a full-time position as a designer for All Points Media. Now, freelancing is his side hustle, doing projects like our book design and layout, while he diversifies his skills and builds his local reputation. Check out his compelling designs at **seanyatescreative.com**.*

project basis or for a limited amount of time. Our clients have had good experiences locally with Mathys+Potestio and 52 Limited.

3. They get clients through Freelance Job Sites.

FREELANCE JOB SITES

These sites are particularly useful if you are new to your career because they provide one solution to the age-old dilemma: How to get experience without experience. They are also helpful for building portfolios—great if you have a wealth of experience from your in-house jobs but want to go freelance and need a robust portfolio to do so.

- **Upwork.com** is the largest player—a behemoth—because of a merger between two competitors. The categories of jobs they offer include Writing, Design & Creative, and Engineering & Architecture.

- **Guru.com** lets you easily showcase your past work experience and offers a daily job-matching feature to make sure you don't miss out on any good opportunities. The Guru Work Room lets you easily manage all your work.

- **Craigslist.com** was started as a job site for creatives in San Francisco. While it has fallen behind as a general job site, it has stayed competitive for creative freelance projects, although you must sift through some low-paying options to find the solid opportunities.

- **99designs.com** allows you to submit designs (like a design contest) to win clients in creative areas like book design, branding, logos, and packaging.

Large freelance job sites, such as **Upwork.com**, include a broad spectrum of freelance work (everything from administrative support to web development) and tend to skew toward the bottom of the market, following the laws of supply and demand. As a rule of thumb, clients more concerned with quality and less with price don't go fishing for freelancers in such large oceans. There are more lucrative, less crowded pools for freelancers through building direct relationships with clients or specialized agencies.

Shop around and build your expertise and portfolio to achieve your desired compensation. You do not need to end up a starving artist!

ENGAGE RECRUITERS AND HIRING MANAGERS

If you've built a community on a social media site, this is an excellent time to increase your engagement with recruiters or managers in targeted organizations.

RECRUITERS

Every job seeker dreams of finding the perfect position and the word *recruiter* often pops up as the go-to person to make that dream happen. While every recruiter is tasked with finding the right person for the job, how they work, whom they work for, and how they're paid varies. It's helpful to understand these differences if you want a recruiter in your job search court.

Internal recruiters (also referred to as "talent acquisition") work in a company's human resources department. While they are looking to fill one or more specific positions at any given time, they're often keeping an eye out for people that might be right for other positions that typically come up at their company.

Here's how to engage internal recruiters:

- ❏ Identify your target company's recruiting team (through their website or LinkedIn) and reach out to them.

- ❏ Find things you have in common. For example, did you go to the same school? Do you share an interest? If so, mention this with enthusiasm when you reach out.

- ❏ Attend events where they're speaking. Say something you noticed about their company or your similar interests, but don't overwhelm them. Do be ready to send them a resume if they ask.

- ❏ If you've built a good online rapport, consider asking them out for coffee.

Staffing agencies or contingency recruiters have a variety of positions they are trying to fill in several companies and are well worth contacting. Keep in mind, however, they are paid only after their client hires a candidate they present. This can go one of two ways: They can be overly enthusiastic and present you for positions for which you might not meet the necessary qualifications. This sometimes happens in high tech. They may tell you, "You're missing a tool? No big deal, you've been working in high tech for 15 years...you're a shoo-in," only to find out from the company that you're not right for the job. Alternatively, they can be extra careful about screening candidates and you might not hear back from them.

Here's how to get the attention of a contingency recruiter:

- ❏ Find staffing companies that specialize in your field. Here are a few in Portland:
  - *Mathys+Potestio* (creatives)
  - *Robert Half* (financial and legal)
  - *Mainz Brady* Group (technical)

- ❏ Submit a focused resume or quick note that highlights a specific type of job in high demand.

  For example, if you are a web developer and you know the latest version of a web tool, you might write to them and say, "Hi, my name is _____. I noticed you have several clients looking for candidates with experience in the latest version of Java and PHP. I recently worked on a project on which I used both these tools."

Retained recruiters are on retainer to fill a select few executive, senior-level, or highly technical positions. These recruiters only want to meet folks who match the relatively small number of positions they are retained to fill (or may be filling in the future).

If you're looking for a senior-level job or have skills that are highly sought after, do the following:

- ❑ Ask folks in your network who have been placed by an executive recruiter to make an introduction.

- ❑ On LinkedIn, search for the word *recruiter* and your specialty. For example, "recruiter AND health care" or "recruiter AND IT." Then reach out to several who interest you.

DEVELOP A POSITIVE RELATIONSHIP

If a recruiter responds or reaches out to you, set up a time to chat. The conversation should be about their needs, not yours. By emphasizing the solutions you›ll bring to the position, the recruiter is more likely to present you to the hiring manager. Stay positive; make them want to keep you in mind and call you if another good match pops up.

It can be discouraging if you work hard to engage a recruiter and still don't get a call back. One of our associates, Janet Brumbaugh, worked as a retained recruiter for 20 years. Here's what she has to say: "I get it, when I was an executive recruiter, I needed to focus my time on satisfying my retained accounts."

If you don't get a call back right away, don't despair. Hold your head high and know you have great skills to offer! Continue networking to meet recruiters, hiring managers, and those who WILL be your champion.

FIND HIRING MANAGERS

To find hiring managers in companies of interest, search the company on social media sites or see if anyone in your LinkedIn network has them as a contact (2nd-degree contact to you). Once you have identified a hiring manager (or recruiter) engaged with your target company or industry, you will want to follow them on Twitter, connect on LinkedIn, or befriend them on Facebook.

One reason to follow or connect with hiring managers on social media is to build relationships with them so they know you and are aware of your skills when they have openings. Whereas it might take weeks for a job post to show up on LinkedIn or Indeed, you can find out about new jobs instantly as recruiters and managers post or announce them on social media. This gives you a head start to research the company, search your network for other contacts, tailor a resume, and still submit your application within a week to give you a clear, competitive advantage.

Another approach is to learn about a hiring manager's problems and then suggest a meeting to pitch how your skills and ideas could solve these problems. As a result, you could create an unpaid volunteer internship, be hired for a project, or become employed without the company ever posting a position.

 TIME TO GIVE YOURSELF A GIFT!

Take a break from your computer screen and visit the current exhibit at the Portland Arts Museum. If you go on the first Thursday of the month from 5:00-8:00 p.m., it's free!

INTERNSHIPS: POSTED OR SELF-DESIGNED

You may be running into the most frustrating catch-22 for job seekers in a new industry: How can you meet the requirement for industry-specific experience if no one will give you the chance to gain experience in the industry? You don't need to be a student to benefit from interning with a desirable employer.

It used to be that nearly all internships were planned and executed under the umbrella of a college or university. The school set up a win-win relationship with employers. Students could work 10–20 hours per week to gain "real world" learning for 12–15 weeks. These unpaid or minimally paid internships also gave students a way to use professional-level skills and generate references in a specific field. Often, they led to job offers after graduation.

Many nonprofit organizations are following this model. They post announcements for paid and unpaid internships, along with their paid positions, on their websites and other sites such as Mac's List. Organizations know that while a volunteer has a weak obligation to the employer—they can stay for an hour or a year—an internship includes a written agreement about the length of the commitment, duties expected, and supervision provided. In short, it more closely mimics a paid position.

EXAMPLES OF SELF-DESIGNED INTERNSHIPS/ PRO-BONO PROJECTS

Private businesses are not allowed by law to benefit from unpaid labor unless the intern is a student earning academic credit. If you're not a student and would like to gain experience in a private business, these clients show how you can design your own internship or offer pro-bono work in exchange for valuable experience and connections:

- **Alison Wiley**, a counselor, wanted to use her advanced writing skills in a green company. A recommendation from Richard Bolles in *What Color Is Your Parachute* caught her eye: create employment by making a proposal to a decision maker. She followed the strategy of meeting and interviewing the employer, identifying a problem she thought she could solve, and then submitting a win-win proposal in which she offered to do pro-bono work.

Through networking, Alison met the president of a well-established engineering consulting firm committed to sustainability. She was able to obtain a meeting in which she offered to do a pro-bono project on the condition that a position would likely be created for her if her performance was satisfactory. He agreed, and after a few months, she moved from the pro-bono project to becoming an employee.

- **Aron** was a Portland actor whose paid work as a customer service representative was too far from his passion for the arts, particularly theater. His career goal was to work in development and fund raising for the performing arts. He submitted several applications but fell short in matching the requirement for experience in development and/ or knowledge of Raiser's Edge, the fund-raising software most often used in development. He wrote a letter to the theater groups that he most admired, offering his weekly day off to help in development with a large variety of tasks, from writing fund-raising letters to stuffing envelopes.

- **Laura** was passionate about a range of social justice and sustainability fields, and her resume showed a series of short periods of employment and volunteer activities. She was able to review her values and commit to the following broad professional mission: "My mission is to help foster job creation through green-collar jobs, sustainable business, or sustainable agriculture." With this strong focus, she identified a dozen nonprofit organizations with similar missions. She selected two for potential internships and sent them the letter shown in *Sample Request for Internship*.

The second example was of someone who approached a friend who was starting a small construction company. She asked the friend if she could do a three-month marketing campaign for $100 (an honorarium, rather than a true salary).

SAMPLE REQUEST FOR INTERNSHIP

Mr. Tom Doe
Sustainability for the Common Good
1234 NE 139th Avenue
Portland, OR 97000

Dear Mr. Doe:

I am writing to offer my skills to Sustainability for the Common Good (SCG) with the purpose of completing a self-designed internship. I call this an internship rather than volunteer work because I can offer a steady commitment of 20 hours per week for several months without pay, with the goal of furthering my professional development. I am available to work either from my home office or at a workplace of your choice.

As you can see on my resume, I have three years of progressively responsible experience in small business administration. I am a highly self-directed individual, able to recognize an unmet need in an organization and take the initiative to create appropriate solutions. I have coordinated a coalition, performed street outreach, planned and implemented a successful press event, created curricula and taught classes on various topics for diverse audiences, and founded a craft cooperative in a developing country.

I am interested in using and further developing several of the following skills:

•**Sharing Information**
 Education
 Outreach
 Public speaking

•**Facilitating and Connecting Groups**
 Meeting facilitation
 Creating mutually beneficial connections between organizations
 Planning, implementing, and following up on programs or projects

•**Organizing and Analyzing Data**
 Creating and analyzing databases and spreadsheets
 Researching and writing business plans and project proposals

I have selected SCG because the mission and goals of the Sustainable Works Campaign resonate with my mission of promoting a sustainable economy through job creation. I would love to do everything I can to help this project take flight.

In return for my unpaid labor, I would ask for a commitment of at least one hour of supervision or guidance per week. I would also appreciate the opportunity to participate in or observe select staff meetings or trainings.

My greatest strength as an employee is that I am both detail-oriented and a people person. For example, I enjoy talking to people in educational and public speaking situations, but also excel at organizational tasks such as creating spreadsheets and reports. My references will attest to my strengths: I am committed, organized, have a strong work ethic, and am friendly and fun to be around.

Please let me know if there are any unmet needs with which I can assist you. I will follow up on this letter within one week. If you have no need at this time but are aware of other associates or friends who might be looking for an intern with my skills and interests, please forward the enclosed resume to them. I appreciate your time considering this win-win proposal.

Sincerely,
Alison Wiley

JOB SEARCH FOR THE OLDER CANDIDATE

VICKI'S STORY

Vicki was in her fifties when she began searching for a part-time job with benefits to complement her true passion to build her practice as a career counselor. Despite her expertise in the career search process, she often felt frozen. As an older job seeker, she had no doubt that she had more to offer than her younger counterparts. It was hard to stomach that she had to mute some of her strengths, particularly her independent nature, to successfully play the game and land a job.

As an older professional, you might feel insecure about your ability to compete with younger candidates for jobs. Some of our older clients harbor some resistance to changing their appearance, language, mannerisms, and approach to accommodate what may seem like a process biased toward younger and less experienced hiring managers. Given the time and effort you've put into your career, these feelings are understandable. Being over 50 ourselves, we are right there with you!

Ageism is insidious and difficult to confront for two reasons: First, hiring managers know that it is illegal to bring the subject out in the open. Second, in their young hearts, they do not believe they are prejudiced. Their biases may be entirely unconscious—their reactions toward older candidates might be dismissive and they may have no idea they are coming across that way. Or, they believe it is logical to be concerned; they think they are acting in the best interest of the company because older people will do the following:

- Miss more work and/or poop out just when the company is facing a dragon deadline—there is a belief that older workers don't have the energy younger workers have.

- Act like a company mommy or daddy and tell others what to do with a wagging finger.

- Want to do it the way it has always been done.

- Not be able to keep up with new trends, especially technology.

- Want more money than what is being offered.

- Have a lower level of enthusiasm for the job, get bored, and then leave or retire too soon.

To prevent employees from leaving too soon, the "clairvoyant" manager thinks it is best not to hire them. Apparently, they have not read the research that shows no correlation between age and job performance.

LABOR SHORTAGES WORK TO YOUR ADVANTAGE

According to the Oregon Department of Employment, many employers are beginning to seek older candidates because of their perceived work ethic. Some employers are moving away from hiring millennials who want "too much" work-life balance or are looking for quick promotions. Also, age bias in hiring is diminishing due to demographic trends. Baby boomers are staying with their employers into their 60s and employers are delighted because of the labor shortage in highly skilled professions.

According to the latest research, the following job sectors are expected to face a shortage of talent through 2025:

- Skilled trades, including electricians, machinists, and welders

- Health care, including occupational and physical therapy aides

- Manufacturing, including production workers and engineers

- Sales, including professionals with a solid combination of social and cognitive skills

- Math-related fields, including actuaries and statisticians

If you are highly skilled in one of these fields, you most likely will be in high demand at any age.

CONSIDER EMPLOYERS WHO SERVE THE ELDERLY

These employers are more likely to welcome more mature workers. Margaret, a job seeker in her early 50s, struck out in interviews for positions as a benefits manager at young tech start-ups before switching her focus to human resources positions at senior communities and in health care.

If you are in a field where technology is quickly evolving, make it your priority to take an online course to bolster your skill level. Research Forbes' list of technical skills which include knowledge of AI and cybersecurity for technology, social media for communications, and Big Data for business forecasting.

FIND AGE-FRIENDLY EMPLOYERS

You can increase your chances for success by researching employers who are typically friendly to older workers. Consider a casual visit to the place of business, ask people in your network, and review photos on company websites to see if there are any older faces. Look up the company on LinkedIn and view the employee profiles and their photos. If there is nary a gray or bald head, your chances of receiving a warm welcome are diminished.

Here are two websites we recommend for older candidates looking for age-friendly employers:

1. The American Association for Retired Persons (AARP, **aarp.org**) lists national employers who welcome older workers.

2. **RetirementJobs.com** has a Certified Age Friendly Employer (CAFÉ) program. This program certifies employers who value employees based solely on their qualification, proficiency and contributions, while also maintaining policies, procedures, and practices that support people approaching or over age 50. Go to their site and create a free account to get a list of CAFÉ employers.

HOW TO COUNTER AGE DISCRIMINATION IN HIRING

To offset possible ageism, remember these tips:

- Only go back 15 years on your LinkedIn profile and the chronological part of your resume (which is also standard practice).

- Leave the dates off your education on the resume.

- Get current on relevant technology, and take off outdated technical terms (Lotus 1-2-3, Mainframe, COBOL).

- Select careers (for example design, writing, and accounting) where selection is driven by work samples or testing.

- Look at services geared toward older people where your ability to relate will be an asset (like hospice nurse, care manager, or sales associate at assisted living facility).

- Carry out a robust networking strategy since the focus on age fades into the background once people get to know you as a person, your enthusiasms, and your skills.

- Adopt a youthful, curious attitude. No matter how accomplished you are in your career, there's always something new to learn from younger people and that can be exciting! If you can adopt this attitude, your youthful nature and enthusiasm will shine through during interviews.

Bottom Line: focus on what you have to offer, not your age. Learn to sell your value in your resume, LinkedIn, and during your interview (review *Interviewing for the Older Candidate.*) Remember, your experience is an asset and your age adds diversity

---

Tip

Get help from your kids or younger friends on clothing choices for networking as well as the interview. Go to the mall and observe how young professionals are dressed. Visit a salon and ban those gray roots from your hair...not only will it make you look younger, it is a pampering gift to give yourself!

Step 3
Prepare Your Resume and Cover Letter

"Don't be afraid to give your best to what seemingly are small jobs. Every time you conquer one it makes you that much stronger. If you do the little jobs well, the big ones will tend to take care of themselves." —Dale Carnegie

When looking for a job, it's frustrating to send out what you think is a great resume and cover letter and get zero response. You may wonder, "What happened? Did they even receive my resume and cover letter? Did they get uploaded into some sort of database, never to be read? Or did my application materials end up in the black hole of the recycle bin?" Truth is, most companies may not even read your cover letter—much less contact you—unless your resume makes the cut.

In this section, we show you how to write resumes that get through to a hiring manager and how to craft a cover letter that gets an employer's attention.

In **Plan Your Resume** we give you an overview of best practices in resume writing and identify outdated trends, which are common mistakes that are easy to make, especially if it's been several years since you wrote your last resume.

Applicant Tracking Software (ATS) discusses the latest software human resources departments use to track employees from the time they apply for a job until they leave. When you apply for a job, your resume will most likely end up in an ATS system which then screens it to see if you are a possible match for the position. We provide guidelines that, if applied, will increase the chances of your resume making the cut.

Knowing how to find the right keywords in a position announcement is a key factor in creating a successful resume. In **Identify Keywords** we use a sample position announcement to show you how to do just that. **Go Ahead—Brag a Little**, an article written for our newsletter by our resume writer, Tifini Roberts, shows you how to write accomplishment statements that highlight your professional qualifications and raise the eyebrows of a prospective employer.

We've included **Accomplishment Statements for Resumes** so that you can see several examples of effective accomplishment statements for different industries. Use the worksheet **Draft Your Accomplishments** to get your brain thinking about how to phrase your most significant career achievements. Write down at least three to five for each recent job, if you can, keeping in mind the requirements in the position announcements.

We've provided several **Sample Resumes** that have been successful generating interviews so that you can see the different approaches and styles to writing effective resumes. **Guide to the Resume Samples** explains how each job seeker put our recommendations into action.

Most resumes are accompanied by a cover letter. Similar to *Plan Your Resume,* **Plan Your Cover Letter** covers general guidelines for writing a compelling cover letter that holds a prospective employer's attention. We've included several **Sample Cover Letters** with different styles and tone so that you can see how cover letters can expand on the best qualities you have to offer a specific employer.

Finally, in **Hold On to Your Optimism and Resilience** we offer comforting words for those times when your resume and cover letter don't yield fruit. Staying motivated after experiencing rejection is difficult, but in this article we help you do just that.

We hope this section will get the resume ball rolling for you. If you are feeling overwhelmed or stuck, remember you can always engage the services of a professional resume writer or coach to help you surmount the roadblocks in your way.

PLAN YOUR RESUME

As you prepare to write your resume, you may be wondering what exactly to include. It is helpful to keep in mind that your resume is simply a one- to two-page advertisement of your education, skills, and work history. Needless to say, it is no easy task to condense all the information into two pages. There are some basic guidelines you can focus on to ensure your resume obtains its goal—landing an interview.

Many career websites state job seekers have as little as six seconds to make an impression with their resume. Other sources suggest 30 seconds is average and, if lucky, up to two minutes. Whatever the number may be, it is not very long. Getting to the point early and specifically is critical to a successful resume.

Let's get to the point here. These general rules apply:

- **Target resumes to the specific open position AND the employer.** Each time you apply for a job your resume should be modified. Yes, this is time-consuming, but absolutely critical.

- **Focus on "What's in It for Them" (WIIFT), otherwise known as audience analysis.** Clearly, state what you have to offer the employer that meets their immediate needs. Employers do not care too much about what you want. They need specific knowledge, skills, and abilities for their success. Show them you are the solution.

- **Use keywords from the job posting and that are relevant to the industry.** Go through the job posting and number all the required qualifications. Then, match them with a corresponding number of your skills and experiences in your existing resume to ensure you capture all the requirements. Demonstrate how you meet each requirement. See *Identify Keywords* for details on how to include keywords in your resume.

- **Share your accomplishments.**
  - Use quantitative examples whenever possible—numbers sell! For example, *Increased widget product sales 20 percent in the first six months at ABC Company, resulting in a $250,000 increase in revenue over the previous year.*
  - Not all accomplishments are numerically measurable. Demonstrate qualitative successes by emphasizing the outcomes that apply to similar situations. For example, *Improved employee retention rates by designing and implementing team-building exercises.*

- **Begin sentences and bullets with action verbs.** Some of the most positively received examples today include: *Achieved, Improved, Trained, Mentored, Managed, Created, Resolved.*

For more information on how to write accomplishment statements with action verbs, see *Go Ahead—Brag a Little* and *Accomplishment Statements for Resumes.*

With all of this great information, you may be wondering, "How do I pull this together?" First, strategize the best format for your current situation and the industry in which you would like to work. There are several ways to organize your resume. The three most widely used include:

1. **Reverse Chronological:** Focuses on employment history and lists experience in reverse chronological order after a brief profile and a few key achievements. This format is most effective when recent work experience is impressive and directly relevant to the target position.

2. **Functional:** Often used when there is a large gap in employment, transitioning to a new industry, or lack of experience. This format deemphasizes individual positions and often does not include dates. Be careful—this format can create concern for employers.

3. **Combination:** Highlights key skills in a Summary section and allows a reverse chronology of job history without too much detail. The summary targets the resume to a specific job and showcases top qualifications.

⛔ OUTDATED TRENDS THAT ARE STILL COMMON MISTAKES IN RESUME WRITING

- **Resumes are one page.** *Not necessarily—only if you have a short work history.*
- **Begin with an objective.** *Nope. That went out of style about ten years ago.*
- **Functional resumes without employment dates are a good option.** *Hardly ever. In this day and age of ATS systems that score your resume based on years of experience, consider this only if you will use your resume as a networking tool or know for a fact that human eyes will be screening your resume.*
- **Use bullets to list job duties.** *Nope—gone are the days of resumes with work histories that read like laundry lists of job duties. Avoid the long bulleted lists of daily tasks and duties. Summarize the job duties in a few lines and save the bullets for the good stuff!*
- **"Responsible for..." is a good way to describe your duties.** *Not so. Begin with action verbs.*
- **"References available upon request"** *goes at the bottom of your resume. No. Provide potential employers your references when requested.*
- **List hobbies at the end of your resume.** *Only if the hobbies are relevant to your target job.*

Now that you determined the most appropriate format, what do you need to include? Figuring out what to include and what not to include are equally important. Remember, a resume is a snapshot of your professional experience, not your life history. Be sure to focus on the most relevant information for the position to which you are applying. Consider the following:

- **The top 1/3 of the resume is the most critical.** Remember you have six seconds to wow the reader and focus on WIIFT—use a profile summary and grab their attention, build credibility, acknowledge the employer's needs, and preview your top qualifications. Add keywords at the top of your resume to help maximize your ATS system score.

- Evaluate the relevance of each **potential section** and determine the appropriate order based on your experience and the employer needs. Begin with a Profile, followed by these potential sections: Work Experience, Education, Certifications, Licensures, Accomplishments, Volunteer Service, and Professional Affiliations.

- Number one rule is to be consistent in your use of **design elements**.
  - Use white space, so your resume does not appear cramped.

- Keep the fonts simple and use only two—one for the text and one for the headings.
- Add a little color, particularly if you are in a creative field.
- Use bullets conservatively—too many are distracting to the eye and eliminates the emphasis or impact of the bullets. The general rule is no more than six.

You've determined the format and narrowed the content to the most relevant, so now how do you submit the document? Submission depends upon if the hiring company will be using Applicant Tracking Software (ATS) or if a human being will be screening your resume. In most cases, resumes are submitted as Microsoft Word or PDF documents and uploaded to the employer's human resource system. If enough keywords are registered, you will get put in the "yes" pile, and a human being will follow up. For more information, see the article on *Applicant Tracking Software*.

A few final words: Always run your resume through the spell and grammar check in Word. Then proofread it at least twice, print it out, read each word following along with your finger, and then read it again backward. Stay positive and be focused on employer needs.

Tip

Make sure you save each version of your resume in a separate file. Doing so ensures you have a collection of great accomplishment statements you can draw from to repurpose your work to apply for future jobs.

APPLICANT TRACKING SOFTWARE (ATS)

Employers often receive hundreds of applications for a single job posting, which can make the recruitment process cumbersome. To manage the large volume of resume submissions, save time, reduce costs, and increase efficiency, employers use Applicant Tracking Software (ATS) to prescreen job applicants. Industry sources estimate that 100 percent of Fortune 1000 companies use ATS systems and 80 percent of small and medium-sized business. By scanning keywords and concepts, ATS systems identify candidates who best match the qualifications for a position, speeding up the screening process and making it easier to meet EEO requirements.

When you complete an online application, upload a resume, or attach a resume to an email, you should assume your materials are going to an ATS system. Even if the organization doesn't use an ATS, an overwhelmed HR assistant is likely to do a quick review of each resume, skimming it for relevant phrases and keywords. They will weed out applicants who don't show on their resumes that they meet job requirements, so it is important to know how to use the ATS to your advantage.

CREATING ATS-FRIENDLY RESUMES

Once you have confirmed that you meet at least 75 percent of the required job qualifications—with emphasis on the first four or five concrete requirements for years of experience, education, and key technical skills—and have thoroughly researched the employer and their needs, you are ready to tailor your resume to get through the ATS screening. ATS systems assign a score to each resume. Those with the highest scores stand the best chance of being passed on to a hiring manager. There are several things you can do to increase the score your resume will receive:

- **Use keywords:** Optimize your resume for each position announcement by using keywords and phrases found in the Qualifications and Job Description sections. Typically keywords describe the education and experience required to succeed in a position. Often they are short phrases, nouns, or adjectives. While the most important keywords are in the position announcement, it is important to research the company's website and social media sites to find more. Use keywords and their synonyms often and throughout your resume to earn more points. Additionally, include industry buzzwords and terms that may not appear in the job announcement. We go into more detail about keywords and where to find them in the next article.

- **Position keywords in context.** Using examples can earn you even more points. When the ATS looks for keywords, they look for context as well as specific words. Avoid fluff words such as *detail-oriented, innovative, team player, or outgoing*.

- **Make sure recent and relevant information appears on the first page.** Information on the first page of your resume will earn more points so be sure to load it with keywords and examples of your successes.

- **Keep the format simple and use white space:** Getting too fancy with fonts and design can confound the ATS. Keep fonts simple. For headings consider Verdana, Tahoma, or Lucinda Sans. For text consider Calibri, Cambria, or Candara. Avoid

Tip

If you are applying for a job in the high-tech industry that requires knowledge of specific coding languages, platforms, databases, tools, or environments, make sure to add a Technical Skills section to the top half of your resume. Don't bury this important information on the second page.

tables with multiple columns. Instead, use tab stops and stick to simple graphics, such as lines, bold, and shading. You can get creative with bullets, using check marks, arrows, or black dots; just be sure to pick one design and stick with it. **Be sure to use white space;** it is as important as keywords because it helps the ATS system know when a new section or past job begins and ends. Use more white space between major resume sections. Bottom line—**be consistent.**

- **Name each resume section:** This is not a time to get overly creative. To avoid confusing the ATS, stick to simple category headings, such as Professional Experience, Technical Skills, Certifications, and Education. Avoid combining major sections. For example, a registered nurse will have Education, Licensure, and Certifications. Each of these needs its own heading so the ATS can categorize them properly.

- **Name your file appropriately:** Currently, Microsoft Word is the most widely accepted format for ATS resume submission. Many ATS systems will accept a PDF. Always upload the document when you are able. When naming your file include your name, the position title, and the company name.

Use these guidelines and you may find that your resume rises to the top and no longer disappears into that notorious "resume black hole." You will increase the chances of your resume passing the ATS screen and getting in front of a human who can evaluate the full range of strengths you bring to the table.

WHILE WRITING YOUR RESUME, GIVE YOURSELF THE GIFT OF MOVEMENT.

Resume writing requires a lot of time sitting at the computer. If it's possible, walk or bike to places you need to go, like the grocery store or the library. If you live near a cafe, walk there for a coffee or tea break. Invite a friend!

Tip

If, when applying for a job online, you are asked to fill in your work history in a manner that essentially mimics the information on your resume, you can be certain the company is using an ATS. In this case, you MUST include keywords from the job announcement when describing your duties and accomplishments. Not sure how to identify keywords? We address this in the next article.

IDENTIFY KEYWORDS

As we've already mentioned, nearly all companies use an Applicant Tracking Software (ATS) system to identify qualified job candidates. Employers program the ATS system to search for keywords and phrases, making the use of keywords in your resume critical to successfully landing interviews. ATS systems search for simple keywords and their use in context. Understanding what to look for, where to find keywords, and how to use them in your resume and other career documents will help you achieve success.

WHAT ARE KEYWORDS?

Keywords are a combination of single words and phrases that encompass a wide range and diversity of knowledge, skills, and abilities used to score an applicant's submitted resume. When looking to identify keywords, know there are several types, including hard skills, soft skills, employment history, and education. Keywords are often nouns, adjectives, and short phrases describing the desired qualifications.

WHERE DO YOU FIND KEYWORDS?

The primary source for identifying keywords is the job announcement. However, your knowledge of the industry, the company's website, LinkedIn presence, and other social media outlets will provide you with a significant amount of information too.

- **Job Announcement:** Review the company overview, job duties, and qualifications by going through each line of the job announcement to look for keywords.

- **Your Knowledge**: Some industries use a significant amount of jargon which is often very technical. These words also may be programmed into the ATS system as keywords. Use your knowledge of your industry to incorporate keywords that will resonate with potential employers and demonstrate your expertise.

- **Company Website:** Review the mission, vision, and values of the organization and notice the language they use to describe themselves and company goals. Use similar words and phrases on your resume to include those keywords. Also, connect the company vision to your values and share that connection in your resume and cover letter.

- **Social Media:** Visit the company LinkedIn profile, Facebook page, and Twitter to see what is happening in the organization. The information you uncover will help you understand their needs, and you can address them in your resume using similar language and terminology, improving your ATS searchability.

HOW DO YOU USE KEYWORDS?

Using keywords throughout your entire resume is imperative. However, it is not enough to simply plop the words into your resume—you want to be strategic about it. Understanding placement, use of word banks, and contextual use of keywords will earn you more points and get your resume to a human reader.

- **Placement:** ATS systems award more points for keywords on the first page of your resume, so you want to be sure to capture as many as possible in the top half of your first page. Given that most HR employees don't have a lot of time to spend reviewing resumes, this placement will help them scan your resume quickly.

Tip

Keep in mind the number of times a keyword or phrase appears in a job announcement does matter. If it appears repeatedly, it is a very important skill for the employer and you will want to emphasize your skills in that area.

- **Word Banks:** Using a keyword bank of the skills you have that meet the qualifications of the job announcement at the top of your resume is beneficial for both ATS systems and human readers. It earns points for the ATS and provides human readers with a snapshot of your skills. Be sure to demonstrate your capabilities later in your resume to prove your ability to meet their needs.

- **Contextual Use:** When writing your profile summary, past job descriptions, and accomplishments be sure to incorporate keywords within the descriptions. These are all areas where you can share examples of your successes and how they will be beneficial to the employer. Each time you apply for a new position these areas may need to be tweaked slightly to incorporate specific keywords.

Bottom Line: Take the time to identify the keywords of each position for which you submit a resume. Employers will not only search for the required capabilities to complete the job functions, they will also want to know that you can communicate with others and which positions you held in the past and where. Some employers may be looking for specific education or training. All of these can be programmed into the ATS system as keywords to screen resumes.

On the following page is a sample job announcement with keywords and phrases highlighted to help you get started.

TIME FOR A GIFT!

Identifying keywords stretches your brain so let's stretch your body as well. Do some yoga or your favorite stretching exercises. If you've never done yoga before, treat yourself to a beginning YouTube yoga video and start out with some easy poses.

Tip

ATS systems are capable of understanding synonyms of keywords. When reviewing job announcements, company websites, and social media pages to research the organization, make a list of all the keywords you find as you go. Once you have a complete list, identify at least two synonyms for each keyword. Using a variety of words will help keep your reader's interest.

SAMPLE JOB ANNOUNCEMENT WITH KEYWORDS HIGHLIGHTED

Job Title: Registered Nurse

Department: Pediatric Hematology—Oncology Clinic & Infusion Center
Location: DCH 10124

WORK UNIT DESCRIPTION

Our pediatric oncologists and cancer experts treat every type of childhood cancer and blood disorder. We are the only comprehensive pediatric cancer center in the region, offering treatments for:

- **Pediatric brain tumors**
- **Blood disorders**
- **Leukemia and lymphoma**
- **Solid tumors**
- **Bone Marrow Transplant**
- **Cellular Therapies**

We recognize that cancer treatment and transplant can create stressful life experiences for children and their families. Children's Hospital offers childhood cancer support resources to help.

WORK SCHEDULE, HOURS, FTE, SALARY RANGE

FTE: .85, Part-time or 34 hours/week

Schedule: Variable schedule initially and with orientation. Anticipated schedule: A mixture of 8- and 10-hour shifts with at least one day off each week of each pay period.

Location: Portland, OR

Salary Range: $38.99-$56.63/hr

Job Type: union represented

FUNCTIONS/DUTIES OF POSITION

The Hematology Oncology registered nurse (RN) provides compassionate, evidence-based, and efficient care to individuals, families, communities and patient populations. The RN's care delivery is consistent with the Oregon Nurse Practice Act, the ANA Scope and Standards of Practice, and the ANA Code of Ethics and meets the standards/expectations of the Nursing Professional Practice Model. In that model, the RN demonstrates the professional role obligations of scientist, leader, practitioner, and knowledge transfer. Professional accountability enriches the RN's engagement as a leader in promoting an interprofessional culture of collaborative decision-making, innovation, lifelong learning, and teamwork.

The Pediatric Hematology Oncology nurse will provide comprehensive care to pediatric hematology/oncology patients in an ambulatory setting, including administration of chemotherapy, blood products, and supportive care. The nurse will need to be certified to administer chemotherapy through the Association of Pediatric Hematology Oncology Nurses (APHON) curriculum. The RN also will provide infusion therapy for specialty service patients such as gastroenterology and nephrology. Also, the nurse will be assigned to coordinate care for two to three Hematology Oncology providers' patient populations.

REQUIRED QUALIFICATIONS

- **Bachelor's of Science in Nursing**
- **Unencumbered Oregon Registered Nursing License**
- **Graduate from an accredited School of Nursing**
- **Strong analytic skills; demonstrated organizational skills; demonstrated problem solving skills; demonstrated communication skills both interpersonal and conflict resolution including fluency in oral and written English; demonstrated planning skills; demonstrated ability to work effectively in a multidisciplinary setting; intermediate computer skills including the ability to send/receive email, navigate information technology associated with the position, and use the Electronic Health Record information and tools.**
- **Previous Experience in Pediatric Hematology/Oncology including administration of chemotherapy and blood products.**
- **Minimum of two years of pediatric nursing experience with acutely ill patients.**
- **Certification in Basic Life Support & Pediatric Advanced Life Support; APHON Pediatric Chemotherapy and Biotherapy Provider**

PREFERRED QUALIFICATIONS:

- **Previous experience with Epic EMR**
- **Previous experience with Epic's Beacon application.**
- **CPHON certification**
- **Internal applicants: BSN preferred**

Want your resume to stand out? **Load it with accomplishments.**

Highlighting accomplishments on your resume is the best way to convey to employers that you are qualified for the job. You are more than your job responsibilities, and accomplishment statements help demonstrate how well you did what you were hired to do. When written properly, they show what you will bring to a prospective employer.

Most people feel a little uncomfortable writing about their accomplishments: it feels like bragging—ugh. The truth is, a little bragging will go a long way to get you noticed by hiring managers. Keep your focus on how your skills and successes meet the needs of the employer; it will help you choose accomplishments directly related to the job announcement.

Now for the fun part: how to write a great accomplishment statement. Using the Challenge, Action, Result (CAR) approach is a simple way to begin. For each position you include on your resume consider the following CAR questions:

- **What challenge(s) did you encounter?** *Global travel and expense systems were outdated and not user-friendly.*

- **What action(s) did you take to resolve the challenge?** *Conducted market research, assessed options, and implemented the new system.*

- **What was the result of your action?** *Saved over $1M in costs, improved efficiency and user experience.*

As you develop your accomplishment statements, there are a few key things to keep in mind:

- Choose accomplishments that are directly relevant to the position and meet employer needs.

- Begin your statement with the result of your actions to solve the challenge.

- Start each accomplishment with an action verb.

- Use quantitative examples whenever possible; numbers are universal and high impact.

- Include keywords from the job announcement. **Example:** *Reduced annual expenses over $1M by implementing new global travel expense system, streamlining processes and improving customer service.*

Having trouble thinking of accomplishments? Ask yourself a few questions to get started. Did you:

- Save money?

- Increase revenue?

- Improve efficiency?

- Build relationships?

- Launch a new product?

- Get promoted?

- Receive an award?

- Take on new responsibilities?

Commit to developing three to five targeted accomplishment statements for each of your past jobs (see *Draft Your Accomplishments* for a worksheet to help you get started). Taking the time to complete this process will help you make a big impression and land interviews.

Bottom line, employers hire people who can demonstrate results, and look to past performance as an indication of the value you offer. So, go ahead—brag a little!

ACCOMPLISHMENT STATEMENTS FOR RESUMES

FOR CREATIVES

- Achieved ongoing media responsiveness by building partnerships with local radio stations.

- Received national award for creating video, audio, and print content targeted to youth-focused environmental "edutainment" platforms.

- Increased sales $10K with an exhibition of paintings, collages, and sculptures in small galleries.

- Stimulated online discussions about social issues with interviews of famous musicians, actors, and activists (including Bonnie Raitt, Joan Baez, and Woody Harrelson).

- Invented video-assist device customized for stop-motion animation which became a commercial product manufactured by Animal Tool Works, Inc.

- Boosted public awareness by 1 million users and engaged 50,000 individuals by overseeing social media campaign from concept to design.

FOR BUSINESS

- Identified new business opportunities with projected annual revenue of $40M by assessing assisted living industry market.

- Reduced postal costs 50% by negotiating a new service agreement with UPS Mail Innovations.

- Increased revenue $500K annually by implementing revised activity-based cost sales plan in collaboration with senior vice president.

- Increased revenue potential by researching and launching wine as a new product line to meet customer requests and satisfaction.

- Reduced cost of goods $450K by negotiating improved logistics incentive programs with top 20 manufacturers.

- Cut costs $600K in three months by orchestrating improved operational procedure of product flow from distribution centers to retail outlets.

- Boosted profits 60% and sales 40% with pioneering marketing approach to the general merchandise dollar category, including full color catalog, containing scanning order capabilities.

- Saved $6M by discontinuing implementation of a midrange merchandising software package.

- Supervised a team of four managers and their direct reports, increasing employee retention through implementing management best practices.

FOR TECHNOLOGY

- Increased website traffic by building promotional landing pages using HTML, CSS and JSPs, and Javascript.

- Chaired Steering Committee meetings to identify and resolve IT and operational issues with minimal impact on customers.

- Prevented future errors with identification of EDI issues and advising carriers to revise processes.

Tip

When writing accomplishment statements for high-tech jobs, it is extremely important to include the required tools, languages, and platforms listed in the job description. This shows the context in which you have used these tools successfully.

- Achieved consistent positive usability test results with new design of user interface using HTML5, CSS3, and SCSS.

- Improved operational efficiency and reduced need for technical support with simultaneous management of 10–15 projects.

- Optimized rapid product delivery by creating proof of concepts and simulations for rapid prototyping of UI, providing design flow for engineers to get immediate UX feedback.

FOR NONPROFITS AND GOVERNMENT

- Earned City of Salem Community Partnership Award by successfully convening and facilitating task-force meetings that addressed complex issues to develop a strategic plan for the City of Salem Senior Center.

- Improved ridership 2.4% annually for five years with educational campaigns, resulting in passage of five-year federal funding reauthorization.

- Gained prominent media coverage for first HIV prevention program in the region targeting African-American gay/bisexual men.

- Enrolled 80 new members in under nine months by implementing unique social service learning program for senior adults.

- Managed $4.5M intercity rail program, quickly acquiring a reputation as both a transportation subject matter expert and a strategic messaging resource.

- Increased membership renewal 7% in two years by tripling annual contact with members.

FOR SOCIAL SERVICES AND EDUCATION

- Awarded Fulbright IIE Doctoral Dissertation Award, Wenner Gren Foundation Predoctoral Grant, and CUNY Graduate School Dissertation Fellowship.

- Earned highest possible evaluations from students, faculty peers, and administrators as teacher and advisor for high levels of support, knowledge, and organization.

- Achieved 80% patient clean and sober rate two years after program completion, highest in center.

- Engaged GED students in preparation for testing by working from their existing knowledge bases and learning styles. Rewarded by observing frustration and learning blocks turn into smiles.

- Increased family reconciliation rates by successfully mediating conflicts between runaway teens and parents.

- Advocated for saving the Human Development Program at Sonoma State University, which served 4,000 students.

DRAFT YOUR ACCOMPLISHMENTS

Think about the jobs you've held and the activities you were most proud of for each one. What was the challenge, the action you took, and the result? Write them down here. When you transfer them onto your resume, lead with the outcome first.

POSITION & EMPLOYER	Challenge/Problem	Action Taken	Result/Solution

Tip

While this chart has room for you to brainstorm accomplishments for every position, it is fine to set a goal of articulating three to five key accomplishments that are most relevant to your future employer. If you get the hang of thinking in terms of your impact, keep going—it will be a tremendous help to have these on hand for your interviews!

Now that you've read our guidelines and recommendations for resumes, it's time to write your own. This task may seem overwhelming—full of uncertainties and second guesses as to whether you are doing it "right." In this article, we summarize our recommendations and show how the samples put them into action so that you can write resumes you will be proud of with minimum stress.

Note: The samples are actual client resumes (we have changed the names). We either wrote them or coached our clients through the process so they could write resumes themselves. In most cases, these clients won an interview!

CUSTOMIZE A COMBINATION RESUME

The top third to half of a combination resume includes a professional summary or profile that highlights your achievements, functional skills, and the skills specific to the duties and qualifications presented in the position announcement. The Professional Experience or Work History section follows with your job titles, employers, dates, and accomplishments.

If you haven't written a resume in over five years, you may think that resumes are either functional (your job duties and accomplishments grouped into skill categories with a brief list of job titles, employers, and dates at the end) or chronological (the jobs you've held and the duties you've performed listed in order from most recent to earliest). Today, nearly all effective resumes are a combination of the best of the functional resume (your relevant skills and achievements) in the Profile or Summary section, with the clarity of the chronological resume (explaining what you did for each employer and when you did it) in the Employment History section.

Note: Notice that each sample resume includes the job title after the name and contact information. This format is

a relatively new trend in resume writing because ATS systems consider the job title to be an important keyword.

Our samples include two valid models, with different style preferences, for the top of a combination resume:

1. After the job title, **Sally Sample, Melvin Model, Rebecca Recruited, and Polly Prototype** each include a brief, one-sentence statement about who they are as a professional (this statement can act like a professional "brand").

   Note: You might want to use this one-line statement as a headline in your LinkedIn profile. See LinkedIn: Create an Effective Profile for more details.

   What follows is a line of relevant keywords from the job announcement. Note that **Nancy Newhire** and **Estelle Example** chose to forgo the branding one-liner and went right to the line of keywords.

   Next comes a professional profile: a brief paragraph no longer than five lines that addresses how you meet the qualifications listed in the position announcement. It includes the number of years of experience relevant to the job and keywords identified in the Duties and Minimum Requirements sections of the job announcement. This section may or may not include a header (**Terrance Technical** uses Profile for this section).

   Note: If you are short on space, simply leave off the header.

2. Instead of a professional statement, paragraph, or line of keywords, **Corey Creative** chose to include a Qualifications Summary as a bulleted list that shows how his experience matches the duties and requirements presented in the job announcement.

No matter how you decide to design or lay out your resume, the top part of your resume should address the position requirements and demonstrate how you meet them. Some industries, however, benefit from the use of a specific approach. For example, **Terrance Technical** works as a software engineer in the high-tech industry. His resume includes a Technical Skills section that lists tools, applications, coding languages, and platforms he knows and are "must haves" for the job.

USE KEYWORDS LIBERALLY

We've emphasized that most employers screen resumes by using an ATS system that searches for keywords and phrases included in the job announcement (see *Applicant Tracking Software* for details). Even if the employer screens resume the old-fashioned way, the HR assistants will review your resume in seconds, also scanning for keywords. Therefore, it's vital to use the keywords and key phrases in the position announcement throughout your resume, as shown in our samples:

- **Rebecca Recruited** and **Corey Creative** include keywords and phrases in the Skills section of their resumes as well as in their job descriptions under Professional Experience.

- **Nancy Newhire** uses keywords to lead off her bulleted list of main qualifications under her Profile paragraph.

- **Estelle Example** grabs our attention with the keyword phrases drawn from the position qualifications, such as *Customer Service Focused* and *Team Collaborator*. Note that Estelle uses additional keywords such as *Confidentiality, Administrative Support,* and *Conflict Management* accompanying each position she held.

- **Polly Prototype** uses keywords such as *Financial Accounting* and *Budgeting and Cash Management* as headers in her functional resume.

- In addition to a Technical Skills section, **Terrance Technical** includes a Tools and Platforms list of technical keywords relevant to each job he held.

- All Samples include keywords and phrases in the Professional Experience sections when describing job duties and major accomplishments.

HIGHLIGHT TECHNICAL SKILLS

As mentioned, technical resumes like **Terrance Technical** generally have a bank of key technical competencies on the first page. Even if you are not in high tech, a job in your field may require specific technical or software expertise as follows:

- **Rebecca Recruiter** is applying for a project coordinator position that lists skills with Microsoft products as a requirement. She includes a Software Expertise section to highlight these skills.

- **Polly Prototype** is applying for a job as an accountant and financial analyst that requires knowledge of industry-specific software such as Oracle and SAP. She highlights these skills in a Technical Skills subhead under her Professional Profile paragraph.

- **Nancy Newhire** incudes her technical skills as the Technology bullet in her list of qualifications under her Professional Profile paragraph.

- **Melvin Model's** resume is for a managerial position that requires or prefers a laundry list of technical skills. Because he is applying for a managerial position, the keyword phrases *Strategic Planning, Budget Management, Operations Management,* and ***Customer Relations*** are most relevant to the job. Therefore, they are emphasized in the top half of the first page while his technical skills are on the second page.

INCLUDE ACCOMPLISHMENT STATEMENTS

The purpose of accomplishment statements is to show your prospective employer the positive impact you had in your previous positions. They should be simple, descriptive, and include a quantitative or qualitative outcome. Lead with the outcome when you can.

Consider listing some of your accomplishments most relevant to your target job at the top of your resume, either as part of your professional profile or in a separate section immediately following it:

- **Estelle Example** lists her relevant accomplishments immediately after her Professional Profile paragraph.

- **Sally Sample** lists her accomplishments in a section called Relevant Achievements, whereas Polly Prototype chose to name the section Selected Accomplishments. Both include the name of the company or organization where they accomplished each achievement.

Consider repeating specific achievements, in slightly more detail, in the Professional Experience section under the corresponding job. Use quantitative outcomes if you are in a field or an industry where dollars and numbers are used to measure effectiveness.

- **Sally Sample's** accomplishments include the following quantitative outcomes:
  - *Increased student retention by 17% with the launch of campus-wide community events...*
  - *Boosted participation by 20% by improving communications between participants and staff...*

- **Corey Creative** lists these quantitative accomplishments:
  - *Saved labor and shipping costs 5–10% in accounts payable by creating administrative system.*
  - *Reduced process payment time 45% by creating a new streamlined process.*

- **Polly Prototype** accomplished the following:
  - *Resolved multiple $100M accounts payable discrepancies by implementing system application controls to match the general ledger...*

Qualitative outcomes can be just as effective in highlighting your accomplishments:

- **Nancy Newhire** includes the following accomplishments:
  - *Reduced meal costs by negotiating with vendors...*

- *Improved student accountability by developing behavior expectations and communicating specific guidelines...*
- *Prevented financial penalties and site shut-down by taking immediate action to coordinate upgrades to achieve compliance...*

- **Melvin Model** accomplished the following:
  - *Streamlined the enterprise reporting environment for Maple County by identifying solutions to eliminate multiple stand-alone systems...*
  - *Increased efficiency of the District Attorney Case Management System by leading a technical team to develop and implement a new automated system...*

- **Terrance Technical** accomplished this while at Hospital School:
  - *Streamlined and improved data access by creating several iterations of Project Management "Console" used by research and technical staff....*

Finally, accomplishment statements can describe awards, accolades, promotions, and feedback, and even include quotes from previous employers:

- **Rebecca Recruited's** resume includes feedback and a quote:
  - *Received consistent positive feedback regarding collaborative skills, enthusiasm for teamwork, and support for coworkers.*
  - *"While working with Rebecca, I appreciated her positive attitude and flexibility in taking on new challenges."—Michael F., Project Manager*

- **Nancy Newhire** *earned two patents for development of competitive products...*

- **Estelle Example** was *Employee of the Quarter for Outstanding Customer Service and Team Initiative*

- **Sally Sample** was *promoted to director of academic advising after one year...*

Tip

To stimulate your thinking about the positive impact you had in your previous jobs, try digging up your performance reviews to see where you stood out, or get together with an appreciative colleague who can trigger your memory.

QUESTIONS AND ANSWERS

No section on how to write a resume is complete without a little Q&A! Here are answers to some questions you might have and how we resolved them in our samples:

1. **What if I've been a freelancer or have had several jobs working for a temp agency? How do I present my work experience?**

While working at other jobs, **Corey Creative** had a side gig as a freelance photographer. If you are a freelancer, address it like you would any other job in your resume, but be sure to list your past clients, especially if there are some heavy hitters among them. For example, Corey's past clients include Airbnb and Condé Nast!

Rebecca Recruited held several job titles as a temporary employee through a variety of staffing agencies. If you look at her resume, you'll notice that she treated each job as if she had been an employee, but simply added via *"name of staffing agency"* after each job title. This format highlights the companies she worked for while being truthful about her actual employer.

2. **What do I do if I've been working, but not recently in my chosen career?**

Estelle Example's resume addresses this situation. Her target job is human resources assistant, yet she has been working outside of the field of human resources since 2005. Here's how she got around this:

- Her professional statement highlights combined experience in HR and administrative duties, many of which are requirements of her target job.

- Her bullets under her professional statement highlight her HR qualifications and experience, even though they occurred over 15 years ago.

- She used human-resources related keywords throughout her resume, even under each nonrelevant job title.

By using this strategy, **Estelle Example** has the perfect combination resume: one that both highlights relevant skills and qualifications and presents work experience in chronological order.

3. **When would I want to use a functional resume?**

A purely functional resume focuses exclusively on skills and job duties, while deemphasizing work history. Functional resumes work well in tandem with in-person networking or informational interviews. They are most useful if you've had gaps in employment or your experience is not obviously relevant or current to the direction in which you want to pivot. If you've had an informational interview or met an influential person at a networking event, you can tailor a functional resume to the specific needs of your contact's company or an open position for which they've put in a good word on your behalf. In this scenario, they may consider you for the job without an ATS screening your resume.

Polly Prototype is an example of a functional resume that highlights her strong accounting and financial management skills while downplaying her gaps in employment—only showing the years and not the months of her various jobs.

USE FUNCTIONAL RESUMES CAREFULLY!

Unless you have a connection inside your target company or already have a foot in the door, we don't recommend using functional resumes because they don't usually make it through an ATS system. The reason is ATS systems measure how many years of relevant experience you've had, and that number is determined by searching for keywords in your Professional Experience section. In a strictly functional resume, your skills may be there, but the years of experience are missing, reducing the chances your resume will make the ATS cut.

4. What if I'm going for a promotion? How do I best present myself?

Melvin Model's and **Sally Sample's** resumes best illustrate this scenario. You'll notice in **Melvin's** resume that, while he has several years of information technology experience, it is at the data, project, and team management level. He is now applying for an assistant director position. Melvin uses a Relevant Experience section to apply the keywords in the job announcement to his experience, demonstrating that he meets the necessary qualifications for the job.

Sally Sample, who is applying for a director of education position, also has relevant experience, although her most recent job title was not at that level and her director-level experience is dated. Like Melvin, she includes a Relevant Achievements section to highlight her qualifications for the position.

WHEN TO SEEK HELP

If you are still feeling overwhelmed and unsure of how to write your resume, you might consider whether or not you are finding the right job postings. The ones that intrigue you the most might not match your skills and qualifications, making it more difficult to put together an effective resume. If this seems to be the case for you, please review *Finding Jobs on the Internet* and *The Best Job Boards* to make sure you are targeting your search correctly.

Know that you can always seek help. However, make sure that whomever you hire is up-to-date on current resume trends and knows how to tailor resumes to specific jobs. Getting an attractive one-size-fits-all resume may be inexpensive and appealing to the eyes, but chances are it will not win you an interview.

Over the years we have helped our clients put together highly effective resumes that have landed them interviews. We're happy to do the same for you!

ESTELLE EXAMPLE

Forest Town, Oregon 97200 ∫ 000-123-4567 ∫ estelle.example@gmail.com

HUMAN RESOURCES ASSISTANT

Problem Solver ∫ Customer Service Focused ∫ Team Collaborator ∫ Clear Communicator

Dependable human resources professional with over 15 years of combined administrative and human resource experience for public and private organizations ranging from six to over 2,000 employees. Accomplished administrative support skills including accurate correspondence, schedule management, filing, and data entry. Skilled at conflict management and resolution in the workplace and known for discretion when handling confidential information.

- ◆ **Human Resources Management certificate and associate of science degree in social sciences.**
- ◆ **Ten years' experience managing human resource matters for over 2,000 employees. [WinCo]**
- ◆ **Led company-wide team of employment coordinators to create process and procedure consistencies resulting in standards manual and improved hiring practices. [WinCo]**

PROFESSIONAL EXPERIENCE

Barista ∫ Coffee Cup Time, Pinecone, Oregon ∫ 2015–Present

Deliver friendly customer service to patrons completing point-of-sale transactions. Train new employees and foster a collaborative team environment that provides superior service by communicating relevant information about order status, product inventory, and special service requests.

- ◆ **Employee of the Quarter for Outstanding Customer Service and Team Initiative ∫ 2016**

Customer Service ∫ Team Collaboration ∫ Inventory Management

Medical Office Assistant ∫ Dr. Martin Jones, DPM, Palm Tree, California ∫ 2014

Acted as point-of-contact for patients providing personable service when answering questions and scheduling appointments. Maintained confidential patient information and records. Managed accounts receivable and payable using Office Ally.

Administrative Support ∫ Confidentiality ∫ Records Management ∫ Customer Service

Customer Care Representative ∫ Ponderosa Pet Rescue, Ponderosa, Oregon ∫ 2012–2013

Greeted and educated customers about animal ownership, adoption, and care. Mentored and trained new staff and volunteers to ensure proper implementation of procedures. Resolved complex communication issues.

Administrative Support ∫ Training ∫ Conflict Management ∫ Customer Service

Manager/Principal ∫ Quality House Services, LLC, Forest Town, Oregon ∫ 2005–2010

Launched, managed, and marketed an eco-friendly house cleaning business servicing over 45 clients. Built strong client relationships resulting in recommendations and increased sales. Supervised, trained, and conducted performance evaluations for six employees. Conducted market trend analysis to remain competitive for product offerings, service rates, and employee compensation.

Recruitment ∫ Negotiation ∫ Employee Training ∫ Payroll ∫ Personnel File Management ∫ I-9 and E-Verify Entry ∫ FMLA ∫ State and Federal Compliance ∫ Workplace Safety ∫ BOLI and EEOC ∫ Confidentiality

Human Resource Advisor ∫ 2001–2005   **Human Resource Employment Coordinator** ∫ 1995–2001
WinCo, Ponderosa, Oregon ∫ 1995–2005

Resolved and managed human resource matters for 2,000 employees including benefits administration, grievance proceedings, employee harassment complaints, employee counseling, security issues, termination, and litigation. Collaborated with management to coordinate employee recruitment, interviewing, onboarding, and training.

Awards : "Heart of the Servant" award
Faith Quest 2004

"Legacy" Award
National conference on youth ministers
Jan 2003

"Honoring Excellence In youth ministry" award
Cascade College, Oct. 25, 2002

"10 years of outstanding service" award
SW church of christ Oct. 2006
"20 years of outstanding service" award
SW church of christ Oct. 2016

PROFESSIONAL EXPERIENCE continued

Human Resource Advisor ∫ 2001–2005   **Human Resource Employment Coordinator** ∫ 1995–2001
WinCo, Ponderosa, Oregon ∫ 1995–2005

Continued:

Set up new employee payroll, personnel files, and ensured compliance with state and federal regulations. Facilitated training for diversity, harassment, sexual orientation, and workplace safety.

- Promoted to human resource advisor.
- **Awarded Certificate of Excellence for external recruiting** ∫ **2004**
- Mentored retail store managers through complicated human resource scenarios including the BOLI and EEOC complaint processes, investigations, and negotiations.

Recruitment ∫ Employment Verification ∫ Onboarding ∫ New Employee Training ∫ Confidentiality ∫ FMLA ∫ Benefits Administration ∫ Payroll Initiation ∫ Personnel File Management ∫ I-9 and E-Verify Entry ∫ Negotiations ∫ State and Federal Compliance ∫ Workplace Safety ∫ BOLI and EEOC ∫ Employee Manuals

EDUCATION ∫ CERTIFICATIONS ∫ TRAINING

A.S., Social Science ∫ Forest Town Community College, Forest Town, Oregon ∫ Expected August 2017

Certificate, Human Resources Management ∫ Mapleton University, Poplar, Oregon

Teacher Certification ∫ Connected Mindfulness School, Ponderosa, Oregon ∫ Expected October 2017

Mindfulness Based Stress Reduction Class ∫ Awaken the Soul, Pine, Oregon

PROFESSIONAL DEVELOPMENT TRAINING

Hiring in Today's Market ◆ *How to Recruit and Retain the People You Want* ◆ *Effective Supervisory Practices*

COMPUTER SKILLS

Microsoft Office: Word, Excel, PowerPoint, Outlook ◆ HRIS ◆ Acquire software and program skills quickly

COMMUNITY ENGAGEMENT

Meditation Leader ∫ Pacific State Prison, Fir, Washington ∫ 2014

Food Packager ∫ Local Food Bank, Forest town, Oregon ∫ 2012

Landscaper ∫ Friends of Big Hill, Birch, Oregon ∫ 2011

Event Volunteer ∫ Helping Hands, Dog Wood, Oregon ∫ 2011

Event Organizer ∫ Save the Farms, Red Wood, Oregon ∫ 2010

[Handwritten annotations:]

Dependable + caring activity planner & volunteer coordinator dedicated to serving youth + senior communities

dedicated+caring A+V coor. passionate who believes in delivery high quality care w/a personal touch

wants to encourage seniors to get the most out of their lives.

Ensures bringing people together from different generations to get to know each other + appreciate each other strong.

—Don't use their exact words

62

Sally S. Sample

Forest Town, Oregon 97000 ◆ 503-123-4567 ◆ sallysample@gmail.com

DIRECTOR OF EDUCATION

Environmental educator dedicated to increasing access to learning for diverse audiences.

Program Management ◆ Grant Writing ◆ Budget Administration ◆ Education Evaluation

Dedicated program manager and educator with 15 years of experience in nonprofit settings, evaluating program effectiveness, implementing improved processes, developing strategic plans, and managing budgets. Collaborative team leader committed to equity and environmental justice. Inspire inclusion of diverse communities with the natural environment through field-based and experiential learning. Established and successful grant fundraiser with a winning record. Skilled networker who enjoys meeting people from diverse backgrounds.

RELEVANT ACHIEVEMENTS

- Managed small and large teams of over 55 staff and volunteers to achieve program objectives and created professional development opportunities for direct reports. **[multiple organizations]**

- Awarded and managed funding expectations of 20 grants totaling nearly $150K supporting environmentally-based topics, including environmental justice, equity, advocacy, and conservation. **[multiple organizations]**

- Developed new programs in collaboration with diverse community partners and multiple college departments to achieve strategic initiatives, including community common reading program **[Hemlock College]** and education abroad program in Spain, focused on environmental issues. **[Douglas Fir University]**

- Oversaw $100K department budget, keeping spending within allotted amounts. **[Hemlock College]**

- Increased retention of students of color and first-generation students by developing a one-on-one advising intervention program connecting students with resources and provided individual assistance. **[Hemlock College]**

PROFESSIONAL EXPERIENCE

Adjunct Instructor   2010–Present

Douglas Fir University, Forest Town, OR, 2010–Present	University of Poplar, Denver, CO, 2011–Present
Maple Community College, Hood River, OR, 2012–2016	The School for Deciduous Studies, Filbert, Spain, 2015

Design and teach environment-society geography and natural resource management courses emphasizing diversity, environmental justice, equity, and conservation. Evaluate program effectiveness and content regularly. Manage diverse student populations with varying needs and support student success in an advisor and mentor capacity. Supervise and provide professional development to research and teaching assistants, including individualized topic training and opportunities to lecture.

- Lead collaborative networking efforts across departments and with community partners identifying student learning opportunities.

Education Abroad Leader/Graduate Editorial Assistant/Teaching Assistant   2007–2010

Douglas Fir University, Forest Town, OR

Handled full-time graduate course load in addition to editorial and teaching assistant positions. Designed layout and edited copy for the *SPAIN: The Journal of the Association for Spanish Studies*. Graded, lectured, and supported diverse student populations with assignments and field-based learning.

- Designed, taught, and led education abroad programs focused on environmental issues in Spain.

© Tifini Roberts, M.S.

PROFESSIONAL EXPERIENCE continued

Director and Assistant Director of Academic Advising   2005–2007

Hemlock College, The Dalles, OR

Managed an academic advising program serving over 2,500 students. Supervised 55+ staff, including direct reports, volunteer faculty, and students, and supported their professional development. Evaluated program effectiveness and implemented policy and procedure changes to increase efficiency and reduce costs. Managed first-year student retention program that improved relations with campus community and augmented cross-department collaboration.

- Promoted to director of academic advising after one year as assistant director.
- Increased student retention 17% with the launch of campus-wide community events for first-year students.
- Improved inter-department communication and efficiency by streamlining course approval process.
- Served as liaison on seven college and university committees because of being identified as a good listener and natural team leader.

International Program Manager   2004–2005

Clear Lake International Exchange Program, Great Lakes, MI

Oversaw non-profit international youth performing arts exchange program. Managed and coordinated team of 20 group leaders, performance staff, and two direct reports, including schedules, student orientation, staff training, and disciplinary actions. Led outreach and recruitment campaigns, including presenting program information to students and families, making follow-up calls, and hosting international performance groups.

- Boosted participation 20% by improving communication between participants and staff and redesigning the record-keeping process.

EDUCATION

Ph.D., Geography, University of Poplar, Denver, Colorado

M.A., Geography, Douglas Fir University, Forest Town, Oregon

M.S., Education: Policy, Foundations, and Administration, Douglas Fir University, Forest Town, Oregon
   Areas of emphasis: **Postsecondary, Adult, and Continuing Education**

B.A., Religious Studies, Juniper College, Pacific Crest, Oregon

PROFESSIONAL MEMBERSHIPS, TRAINING, AND COMMUNITY INVOLVEMENT

Memberships: American Association of Geographers ◆ Association of Pacific Coast Geographers ◆ International Union for Conservation of Nature, Thematic working group on cultural practices in ecosystem management

Workshops: Inclusive and Culturally Responsive Curriculum and Pedagogy (May 2017) ◆ Developing Leadership that Contributes to Racial Equality (June 2017)

Certification: Wilderness First Responder, NOLS, valid through August 2018

Languages: Spanish—intermediate level ◆ Portuguese—beginning level

Community Volunteer: Banks for Kids ◆ Dreams Come True Foundation

Melvin Model

Treeville, Oregon 97000 | 503-123-4567 | melvinmodel@gmail.com

ASSISTANT DIRECTOR INFORMATION TECHNOLOGY

"There is always a solution to problems whether it's changing business processes or identifying technical improvements." ~ Melvin Model

Strategic Planning | Budget Management | Operations Management | Customer Relations

Information Technology Manager who articulates vision for the organization, drives strategic execution, and engages direct reports in delivering high-quality results. Dedicated leader who has spent the last 15 years managing technical teams through the development and implementation of information and telecommunication system design. Takes team-oriented approach to leadership and management encouraging creative ideas and solutions.

Relevant Experience

- Develop long-range strategic plans and lead technical teams to complete large scale/enterprise projects for Maple County, including Sheriff's Office RMS/JMS system [$1.5M budget]; District Attorney Case management system [$750K budget]; Birch County Phone system [$280K budget].
- Create project budgets that align with county goals and objectives and collaborate with IT Governance and leadership to provide expertise and implement agreed upon solutions.
- Manage professional development budgets and plans supporting staff growth and motivation; emphasize the importance of implementing the plans and hold managers accountable.
- Provide frequent project update presentations and interacts comfortably with customers, vendors, department heads, and elected officials encouraging collaboration and transparency.
- Monitor technology trends and identify efficient, cost-effective improvements aligned with organizational strategy and goals.

PROFESSIONAL EXPERIENCE

Maple County Oregon   Treeville, Oregon • 2001–2015

Information Technology Manager, 2014–Present
Manage highly technical teams comprised of county employees and external vendors who collaboratively design, create, and implement complex computer applications. Identify ways to improve department efficiency by developing team goals and objectives, monitoring progress throughout projects and managing project budgets. Provide leadership and technical expertise, negotiate vendor contracts, and represent the county, acting as liaison with vendors. Support professional development of staff and encourage creative solutions to technical projects.

- Step into the IT Director AIC (Acting in Capacity), when the current director is away, to manage the budget and ensure departmental functions continue to operate smoothly.
- Prioritize existing customer projects for six to seven departments meeting monthly to strategize their IT needs.
- Manage and lead a team of GIS staff responsible for developing and implementing a five-year technology roadmap to sustain GIS architecture in collaboration with GIS Directing Committee using customer feedback.

Information Technology Project Manager, 2001–2014
Led and directed teams that supported technical projects upholding countywide goals. Determined scope and priority of projects and hired contractors following county contracting guidelines. Identified project team members and managed performance providing leadership and technical support. Acted as liaison between Maple County departments providing the best possible technical solutions to requests. Managed budgets ranging from $280K to $1.5M and presented project updates to management and stakeholders.

- Developed a project management methodology improving transparency and accountability between departments.
- Streamlined the enterprise reporting environment for Maple County by identifying solutions to eliminate multiple stand-alone systems and led technical teams, managing all aspects of project development and implementation.
- Increased efficiency of the District Attorney Case Management System by leading a technical team to develop and implement a new automated system that is currently in use—12 years later.

PROFESSIONAL EXPERIENCE continued

Pacific Fisheries Company   Forest Town, Oregon ▪ 1994–2001

Data Manager, 1998–2001

Oversaw the development and maintenance of the central database for the Northern Fisheries Information Network to manage marine fish in Northern waters. Coordinated with state and federal government agencies ensuring smooth data acquisition. Led special projects and created software requirement specifications for new data entry applications.

- Improved data collection efficiency by creating an automated program for submission of the Northern portion of the Fisheries of the United States report for the National Marine Service.

Assistant Data Manager, 1994–1998

Developed relational databases to share information between agencies collaborating on a multi-state effort to compile collected data about anadromous fish in the Northern Water Basin. Managed the ongoing maintenance of databases and developed cross-referenced files to generate reports. Built rapport with private and public requestors.

- Represented PFC at community events to inform and educate the public about regional fisheries issues.
- Led Dungeness crab quality testing, including supervising observers, documentation, and boats; submitted timely reports impacting season opening of multi-million-dollar commercial crab fishery.

EDUCATION

B.S., Fisheries Science, Douglas Fir University, Birch, Oregon

SELECTED PROFESSIONAL DEVELOPMENT

Records Management, Retention, and Destruction Seminar, 2010

Electronic Records Management Seminar, State of Oregon, 2009

ISO20000 training, 2008

Project Management Certification, State of Oregon, 2007

Microsoft SQL Server Reporting Services Administration, 2004

TECHNICAL SKILLS

Uniquely positioned to manage the Information Technology department and support staff to achieve strategic goals, with first-hand experience and in-depth technical knowledge of the Maple County systems.

Management Leadership: Maple County Management Development series

System Administration: SQL server reporting services, District Attorney Case Management system, Building Inspection Permits Plus, MS MIIS Identify Integration server

Operating Systems: XP, Windows 2000, Windows 7, Windows 10, Unix

Languages: PowerBuilder, ArcView GIS

Methodologies: ITIL, ISO20000, Project Management Institute, Agile, Scrum, System Development Life-Cycle

Software: MS Access, SQL, PL/SQL, .net

Relational Database Management Systems: MS SQL Server, Oracle RDMS

Tools: Microsoft Reporting Services, FTP

Polly Prototype

Douglas Fir, Oregon 97000 | 503-123-4567 | pollyprototype@gmail.com

Accountant | Financial Analyst

"I create, build, and implement financial solutions." ~ Polly Prototype

Audit Review | Process Improvement | Project Management | Budgeting | General Ledger Management

Reliable and ethical Financial Analyst/Accountant with over 20 years' experience in all phases of financial accounting, planning, and reporting. Excellent analytical skills and ability to communicate complex financial data in easy-to-understand terms. Comfortable operating in fast-paced environments prioritizing and managing multiple detail-oriented projects. Equally effective at working on projects requiring independent attention or team collaboration.

Technical Skills

Advanced Excel | Advanced Access | Word | PowerPoint | Oracle | Discoverer | Cognos | TM1 | Hyperion | SAP

Selected Accomplishments

➤ Resolved multiple $100M accounts payable discrepancies by implementing system application controls to match the general ledger in collaboration with the Information Technology department. **[ABC, Inc.]**

➤ Improved accuracy of financial schedules for employee benefits system by developing and maintaining complex formulas that combined history and current accumulated transactions. **[ABC, Inc.]**

➤ Established improved system processes to generate financial statement balances that helped management support the system upgrade and implementation of Oracle, including A/R, A/P, fixed assets, tax, posting reference, liabilities, equity, and accountable for foreign exchange and consolidations. **[ABC, Inc.]**

➤ Developed annual operating budgets and five-year capital plans to manage and improve rental properties. **[JKL Co.]**

➤ Created bank statement system to accurately record controlled EFT receipts and disbursements. **[DEF Group]**

Key Accounting and Finance Qualifications

Financial Accounting

➤ Managed and reconciled monthly general ledger accounts, including working capital and PPE analysis for multi-component large organizations.

➤ Maintained accurate journal entries and developed and implemented improved fund account systems.

➤ Streamlined and enhanced accounting, report, and analysis techniques for accruals, external GAAP, and compliance.

Financial Planning, Analysis, and Reporting

➤ Created, interpreted, and reported financial information in support of general business operations and long-term strategic planning functions, including add income, property, franchise, payroll, sales and use, tax analysis, internal control monitoring, accruals, deferred assets and liabilities, and expenses.

➤ Prepared and presented monthly financial statement package to management teams, including P&L, balance sheets, and cash flow.

➤ Resolved transaction discrepancies for A/R monthly and year-end audits for multiple scenarios with major value impacts over $100M, resulting in recommending improved processes and controls meeting SOX compliance for accurate external reporting.

Budgeting and Cash Management

➤ Prepared multi-national budget forecasts and corrected budget variances in multiple financial environments, including large corporations, small businesses, and government research projects.

➤ Recommended and implemented improved variance analysis and expense forecasting methods.

➤ Monitored and reconciled cash position with financial institutions and provided accurate and timely Treasury control and reporting reviews affecting assets, liabilities, and expenses.

Polly Prototype

Professional Experience

Financial Accountant | DEF Group | Maplewood, OR, 2017

Financial Analyst | GHI Organization | Pine, Washington, 2016

Senior Accountant/Financial Analyst | JKL Company | Dogwood, OR, 2010–2015

Senior Accountant/Financial Analyst | MNO, LLC | Cedar, OR, 2008–2009

Accountant/Analyst | PQR Institution | Blue Spruce, OR, 2003–2007

Senior Financial Accountant/Analyst | ABC, Inc. | Redwood, OR, 1990–2002

Education and Certifications

B.S., Accounting and Finance | Maplewood University | OR

Certified Public Accountant | Maplewood Board of Accounting | Current

Certified Associate in Project Management | Poplar Organization | Maplewood, OR

Masters Certification in Business System Analysis and Project Management | TUV University | Cedar, OR

Certified Management Accountant | XYZ Institute | Emerald City, WA

> ➤ Advanced Coursework: Financial Reporting ▪ Statement Analysis ▪ Valuation ▪ COSO Internal Control/SOX

> ➤ Advanced Coursework: Financial Planning and Analysis

Business Analysis Certification | BBB Organization | Somewhere, CA | In Progress

Rebecca Recruited

REBECCAJRECRUITED@GMAIL.COM | 503-123-4567 | PORTLAND, OR

PROJECT COORDINATOR

Administrative professional committed to sustainable infrastructure with over five years' experience in project coordination and administrative support.

PROJECT MANAGEMENT | MEETING PLANNING | REPORT WRITING | INVOICE PROCESSING

SKILLS

- Proven success managing competing priorities
- 5+ years office administration experience including bookkeeping, AP/AR
- Coordinated meetings for internal and remote staff and clients + subcontractors

- Consistent positive feedback on drive and ability to learn
- Strong customer service orientation
- Project coordination for energy efficiency evaluation and implementation
- Excellent written and verbal communicator

SOFTWARE EXPERTISE

- Expert: Word, Excel, PowerPoint, Outlook, and Salesforce
- Intermediate: Access, Adobe Illustrator and InDesign, Visio

PROFESSIONAL EXPERIENCE

TopCo Beaverton, OR   **January 2018—Present**
Project Coordinator via Mystaffing

Work across multiple departments, communicating client deadlines and priorities and ensuring quality execution of mass torts claims process. Track bottle-necks and potential slowdowns in expediting complex claims administration process.
- Increase productivity by collaborating with client services team to process a minimum of 75 claimant issues per week.

BestResult Portland, OR   **July—November 2017**
Program Coordinator via Best Staffing

Coordinated all elements of energy efficiency construction and incentive process: verifying audits, verifying eligibility of projects, reporting progress, and supporting project close-out activities. Exercised advanced organizational skills taking on a role without prioritization or communication process in place.
- Streamlined work flow by developing prioritization processes and effective communication protocols.
- Ensured timely deliverables using proactive, assertive project management skills to effectively communicated and coordinate projects with contractors.
- "While working with Rebecca, I appreciated her positive attitude and flexibility in taking on new challenges."—Michael F., Project Manager.

WeLoveKids Portland, OR   **February—June 2017**
HR Field Assistant via We Recruit

Resume coached and edited by Leslie Yeargers, MA

Professional Experience Cont.

WeLoveKids cont.

Utilized strong communication and organization skills to coordinate field HR staff, ensuring internal team requests and priorities were addressed. Resolved employee issues on HR line by initiating call backs and escalating as necessary.

- Increased HR efficiency and employee engagement by resolving employee issues over the phone, reducing the number of escalations to management team.
- Processed severance payments for 400+ employees at more than 150 centers nationwide.

No Risk Insurance   **June—December 2016**
Bookkeeping and Operations Coordinator via We Staff the Best

Resolved issues on complex balance sheet working concurrently with CPA. Persistently researched information necessary for accurate accounts receivable and payable.

- Ensured customer satisfaction by processing timely monthly payments to over 30 different insurance carriers.

We R Consulting, Seattle, WA   **May 2014—February 2016**
Associate Consultant

Conducted data analysis in a fast-paced energy consulting firm, working with energy engineers.

- Increased client satisfaction through timely correspondence with all clients and accurate and thorough presentations to firm's most valuable client.
- Increased quality of data analysis by applying graduate level statistics knowledge and skills.
- Received consistent positive feedback regarding collaborative skills, enthusiasm for teamwork, and support for co-workers.

We R Consulting, Seattle, WA   **September 2012—May 2014**
Administrative Assistant

Established multiple processes and system of documentation as the company's first administrative assistant. Formatted and proofread reports, memo, and presentations. Demonstrated flexibility, adaptability and positive attitude in fielding request from executive team and consulting staff.

- Streamlined company processes by exercising initiative in problem solving regarding incentive cards sent to utility customers, fielding customer complaints, tracking card issues, and eventually finding and selecting new card vendor.

We Cover You Insurance, Lake Stevens, WA   **April 2011—September 2012**
Customer Service Representative

Assisted company president in managing bookkeeping practices.

- Increased customer satisfaction by developing a more responsive and comprehensive system of responding to client policy changes and requests.
- Took on the management of a two-month long implementation of new Client Management System, including buy-in from staff, extensive troubleshooting, and issue tracking.

EDUCATION
Smith College, Northampton, MA   B.A. Anthropology/Government 2008
Dean's List 2005-2008

Nancy Newhire

My City, Washington 98685 ◆ 123-456-7890 ◆ newhire@email.com

Engineer

Regulatory ◆ Environmental ◆ Quality ◆ Chemical

Results and people-oriented engineer with master's degree in chemical engineering (Stanford) and over ten years' experience leading detailed projects and building functional teams. Outgoing persona and not afraid to ask questions or cold call people to learn what is needed to reach goals. Equally comfortable working independently or with collaborative teams with knack for resolving issues and achieving win-win outcomes.

- **PROJECT MANAGEMENT:** demonstrated skills to oversee projects of all sizes from inception to completion while managing budgets and achieving desired outcomes including waste water treatment projects
- **RELATIONSHIP MANAGEMENT:** built trusting long-term relations with networks of volunteers and vendors to support program goals, and engage cross-functional teams in developing accurate and efficient processes.
- **REGULATORY AND COMPLIANCE:** exhibited dedication to detail-oriented management of data and regulatory compliance expectations to remain within state, federal, and local laws within a complex manufacturing facility
- **QUALITY CONTROL:** conducted thorough analysis of data and procedures to ensure safety and top-quality products for customers and projects.
- **TECHNOLOGY:** Microsoft Office Suite | Google Suite | Dropbox | Cloud-Based Document Management

Experience

Logistics and Event Manager, BestBots Robotics Team
Robot High School | My City, Washington | Seven Years—Present

Lead program management and logistics for robotics competition assisting 50+ students. Promote program, mentor students, and present specifics to parent and volunteer audiences. Oversee budget and expenses for 100+ people, including travel and event organization. Coordinate 20+ adult mentors and additional volunteers to staff events and raise funds. Establish and maintain network of individual and business relationships to support program and keep costs low.

- **Reduced meal costs** by negotiating with vendors and establishing long-term relationship.
- **Improved student accountability** by developing behavior expectations and communicating specific guidelines to students and parents.

Environmental Manager
Big HABA Co | Big City, Texas | Six Years

Managed and maintained federal, state, and local compliance, for air, water, and waste permitting. Monitored large equipment and site storage, including boilers, cooling tower, roasters, underground storage tanks with volatile chemicals, and wastewater ponds. Oversaw change management with assessment of processes and evaluating impact to site permits. Implemented improved processes and procedures based on detailed analysis to maintain efficient operations. Built relationships with internal and external stakeholders to resolve issues and implement changes collaboratively. Established audit compliance team and maintained detailed and meticulous files for audits.

- **Reduced costs of wastewater pond upgrades** with creation of technician team focused on developing solutions to reduce solid and liquid waste.
- **Resolved resident complaints and reduced wastewater treatment pond odor and foam issues** by analyzing aeration level data and hiring a consultant to implement changes.
- **Prevented financial penalties and site shut-down** by taking immediate action to coordinate upgrades to achieve compliance with newly discovered regulations for underground storage tanks.
- **Achieved site compliance** with implementation of proper disposal procedure for fluorescent lights with mercury.
- **Delivered site training** as required by permits and environmental regulations as well as D.O.T. training

Experience continued

Chemical Engineer
ChemicalCo | Wood Park, California | Five Years

Supervised multiple projects for nonprofit contract research development company focused on STEM fields and business. Coordinated details and sustained relationships to meet client needs for governmental agencies, such as DoD, DOE, and EPA to commercial clients looking for competitive advantages. Researched with extreme accuracy, including lab testing, quality control, record management, data analysis, and interpretation. Wrote reports and presented outcomes to clients to generate new business. Collaborated with internal teams to complete projects and achieve goals.

- **Earned two patents** for development of competitive products that improved abrasion resistance for laminate countertops.
- **Created portable water "concentrator"** utilizing reverse osmosis to concentrate chemicals and delivered functional product to EPA, along with operational documentation, to detect pollutants below detectable levels in streams, rivers, and other water bodies.
- **Developed program and testing of dry powder inhalers,** with cross-departmental collaboration to measure lung penetration of prescription medicines using fluorescein requiring significant chemical handling and data analysis.

Education

MS, Chemical Engineering | Engineering University, Big City, California
Area of Emphasis: **Environmental Engineering**

BS, Chemical Engineering | University of BigWoods, Davis
Area of Emphasis: **Bioengineering**

Volunteer Engagement and Board Memberships

Volunteer
My Favorite Youth Equestrian Ranch | My City, Washington | Four Years—Present

Improved client experiences with creation of streamlined procedures ensuring consistent customer expectations. Utilized cloud-based system to upgrade volunteer management system from paper and pencil.

Volunteer
My Favorite Youth Equestrian Team | My City, Washington | Two Years—Present

Advised equestrian team and organized facilities. Organized fundraisers and communicated schedule to team.

President
Robot High School, Math and Technology Magnet Booster Group | My City, Washington | Two Years

Led and organized Hands-on-Science Night event raising $5K and increased volunteer participation and student support.

Coach
My Favorite Team | My City, Washington | Five Years

Launched and coached team for five years. Managed program implementation and operations. Handled parent and student relations resolving issues with patience and understanding.

Board Member, PTA
Neighborhood Elementary and WERSchool Middle Schools | My City, Washington | Five Years

Developed financial management tracking procedures for Scrip fundraiser and established free morning math tutoring.

Corey Creative

Pasadena, CA 91106 | coreycreativephoto.com | 123.456.7890

Photographer & Content Manager

QUALIFICATION SUMMARY

- Over 20 years of photography experience as a photographer, producer, digital asset manager, and editor.
- Over 15 years working with art directors, talent, prop, food, and wardrobe stylists.
- Expert knowledge level of film-based and digital photography.
- Strong client/customer services with a focus on collaboration and building trust quickly.
- Attention to detail, very organized and over 5 years' experience creating complex systems.
- Self-starter with a focus on efficiency and identifying operational improvements.
- Drives organizational change by being adaptable and focusing on teamwork.

SKILLS

- Film & Digital Photography Systems & Processes (35mm, Medium & Large Format Cameras)
- Vendor Management & Distribution
- Microsoft Word & Excel
- Adobe Photoshop Creative Suite

- Digital Asset Management
- Lighting (Natural, Strobes, Fluorescent, Tungsten)
- Adobe Lightroom
- Adobe Bridge

PROFESSIONAL EXPERIENCE

PHOTOGRAPHY | Los Angeles, CA & Portland, OR
Freelance Photographer

1999 - Present

Photographer for travel, food and lifestyle magazines, including high-end hotels, businesses, restaurants and cookbooks. Negotiated licensing, fees, expenses, and contracts with clients. Managed and track digital files. Contributed to a Nautilus Book Award cookbook called "The Rawvolution Continues…"
Photography clients include:

- Airbnb
- Conde Naste Traveler
- Coastal Living
- Vegetarian Times

Freelance Producer | Digital Asset Management | Editor

2013 - Present

Edited, color corrected and archived digital images for multiple photographers. Consulted on contracts and bids with various photographers.

- Produced photoshoot for CharBroil Grills managing crew of 15-18 people spanning 7 days.

SUNSET MAGAZINE | remote from Los Angeles, CA

2009 – 2013

Sunset is one of the most prestigious magazines in the West focusing on home, travel, gardens and food.
Staff Photographer

- Delivered beautiful, creative images within the aesthetic of Sunset as a travel photographer.
- Met publication timelines by adapting to changing location, story, and logistics requirements.
- Organized all aspects of travel within a budget and tracked monthly expense reports.
- Managed a variety of projects by coordinating details with Directors and Editors in home office.
- Managed, routed and tracked thousands of digital assets monthly.

GREEN ZEBRA GROCERY | Portland, OR

1/2015 – 9/2017

Adapt to constant change and create systems to assist in scaling operational procedures for a grocery store that expanded from 1 to 3 stores in less than 3 years. Delivered great customer service daily to bring healthy food and inclusive culture to everyone as part of Green Zebra's mission.
Green Zebra Grocery: Accounts Payable Steward, (4/2017 – 9/2017)

- Resolved discrepancies by communicating with 15 managers and directors and 20 to 40 vendors.

Resume written by Ursala Garbrecht

Green Zebra Grocery continued...
- Ensured accurate accounts payable using Quickbooks and Excel for 3 high volume stores.
- Saved labor and shipping costs 5 – 10% in accounts payable by creating administrative systems.
- Reduced payment process time 45% by creating a new streamlined process.

Green Zebra Grocery: Lead, Front End & Barista (6/2016 – 4/2017)
- Streamlined front end operations by facilitating communicating strategy for up to 10 staff.
- Individually trained 19 new staff in barista skills and assisted with cashier training.
- Optimized teamwork by updating task list and implementing changes for all front-end staff.

Green Zebra Grocery: Lead Barista (9/2015 – 6/2016)
- Ordered supplies from vendors weekly by assessing department needs.
- Assisted the Front-End Manager by creating new checklists for training.
- Updated ordering systems and remade forms to streamline workflow and create less waste.
- Introduced a new tea program by initiating vendor, analyzing prices, and promoting products.

TE AMO ICE CREAM | Los Angeles, CA   2012 – 2014
Owner / Producer
- Launched an artisanal ice cream business by creating a quality product and an exciting brand.
- Created imagery to promote the brand.
- Tracked profitability, inventory, vendors, costs, pricing and customer base using Quickbooks.
- Expanded brand and customer base by promoting on Instagram and targeted MailChimp emails.
- Grew business by developing partnerships, vending private events, and developing community.

EDUCATION

Art Center College of Design | Pasadena CA
     Bachelor of Fine Arts in Photography

Terrance Technical

503-123-4567 | terrtech@comcast.net

Senior Software Design Engineer

PROFILE

Innovative and quality-driven Senior Software Design Engineer with expertise in full-stack development and architecture on a wide variety of projects, platforms, and applications. Five years of DevOps, systems and network design/management experience.

TECHNICAL SKILLS

Languages	Java, C++, PHP, HTML, Ruby, Javascript, Go, Perl
Databases	MySQL, Postgres, Redis, Cassandra, BigQuery, Neo4J, SQLite
OS	Linux(CentOS, Debian), OS X, Windows, Android
Cloud	Google, AWS
Tools	Kafka, Kubernetes, Docker, RabbitMQ, Datadog, Kinesis, SQS, JQuery, GIT, JIRA, Agile, Flink, Puppet, Memcached, Nagios, Bamboo, Jenkins

PROFESSIONAL EXPERIENCE

Web Speed | Senior Software Engineer   4/16 - 1/18
Worked in Data Services group to process and store high-volume inbound client metrics.
- Lead development of Kafka based streaming pipeline for data ingest.
- Rewrote legacy monolithic system as Kubernetes micro Web services.
- Conducted research on anomaly detection.

   Tools and Platforms: Java, JUnit, Postgres, Redis, Kafka, AWS (EC, SQS, Kinesis, S3), Google Cloud(Kubernetes), Datadog, Bamboo, Go, Python, BigQuery, Cassandra

BigData.com | Senior Software Engineer / APM Data Services   3/15 - 4/16
Worked in Data Services group to develop and maintain high-volume monolithic systems and microservices.
- Developed proof-of-concept for graph-based accounting system using Neo4j; replacement dashboard for legacy APM system; and for a system to enable discrete billing for cloud-based systems using Kafka, Storm, Flink and Cassandra.
- Wrote microservices-based billing system.

   Tools and Platforms: Java, AWS, JUnit, Kafka, Docker, Redis, Memcached, Cassandra, Neo4j, Storm, Flink, Jenkins

Hospital School / Department of Bio Engineering   4/06 – 3/15
Research Associate
Sole developer for majority of We Care Laboratory (WCL) technical needs. Worked with faculty, staff and students to design and develop software and hardware solutions. Projects had diverse hardware requirements such as Zigbee sensors and WiiFit balance board. Reverse engineered commercial products.
- Created system to securely gather and store data from hundreds of in-home networks of behavioral sensors.
- Streamlined and improved data access by creating several iterations of Project Management "Console" used by research and technical staff to monitor subjects and systems for research.
- Wrote "Puppet wannabe" to keep Windows XP clients updated.

Terrance Technical

PROFESSIONAL EXPERIENCE continued

Hospital School / Department of BioMedical Engineering   4/06 – 3/15
Research Associate

Continued:

- Designed and implemented kiosk-based video chat system to track all communications, clients, recorded video and audio streams on centralized server.
- Trained and mentored junior staff.

    Tools and Platforms: C/C++, Java, PHP, Perl, MySQL, Windows XP, 7, Linux (CentOS, Debian), Android, Visual Studio, Eclipse, Red5, Ruby, Neo4j, RabbitMQ, Puppet, Xuggler, Cassandra, JQuery

Hospital School / Department of BioMedical Engineering   4/10 – 3/15
IT Specialist
Sole provider of DevOps for Point of Care Laboratory. Managed all hardware, networking, and server software. Used combination of real and virtual systems to provide all databases, file storage, networking, and email in support of group research projects.
- Owned all aspects of two datacenter moves for POCL equipment, including racking, network/switching topology, and ongoing 24/7 maintenance.
- Streamlined IT by managing systems, sharing software installations, and providing general technical support for Bio Engineering department. Included email, account management, networking, tape backups, VMWare and generalized systems maintenance. Systems included servers from Dell, Digiliant and EMC.
- Assisted in transition of systems and processes to campus-central IT group.

    Tools and Platforms: Linux (CentOS, Debian), Windows (XP, 7 and Server 2012), Xen, DRAC, VMWare, EMC, Equallogic, Sendmail, Nagios, Postfix, DNS/BIND, MySQL, Puppet, Neo4j, Cassandra

Freelance Projects   12/02 – 4/06
- Designed and implemented web-based software using Java/Tomcat for managing monthly shift schedules for emergency room physicians.
- Designed and created web-based auction software to purchase tickets, manage guests, track sales, and generate receipts.
- Created web-based software using Java/Tomcat to create online photo albums with multiple navigation paths, online editing and sales.

ADDITIONAL EXPERIENCE

Mega Computer Corp | Associate Developer   4/01 - 12/02

Mega Software Corp | Software Design Engineer / Lead   6/94 - 4/01

EDUCATION

Bachelor of Arts | Non-Technical University in Mytown, USA

RESUME CHECKLIST

We covered a lot of information about creating a resume, so let's simplify it with a quick checklist.

My resume:

❏ Includes a heading with my name in large font and contact information in a smaller font.

❏ "Wows" the reader in the top 1/3 of the page and maintains interest to the end. Communicates key strengths for the position in a Profile or Summary of Qualifications section.

❏ Includes current work experience—typically the past ten years. Does not include anything over 15 years unless it is specifically related to the target position.

❏ Is packed with industry-specific language and keywords to ensure it is ATS-friendly.

❏ Includes outcomes and accomplishments to show what I've done and how well I've done it. These can be either quantitative (% increase, $$ saved, etc.) or qualitative (improved morale, reduced waste, improved efficiency, etc.).

❏ Focuses on the needs of the position/employer and how I meet them.

❏ Uses varied action verbs and powerful statements.

❏ Contains impeccable grammar, spelling, sentence structure, and punctuation.

❏ Communicates crucial transferable skills.

❏ Is available in the appropriate document formats: Word (.doc, .docx) or PDF.

❏ Is appealing to the eye, easy to read, and uses consistent formatting—uses the most effective resume format, modern fonts, graphical elements, and white space.

❏ Minimizes any potential concerns such as gaps in employment or recent graduate.

❏ Eliminates dates of education to avoid ageism.

❏ Has been proofread at least twice—spell and grammar check in Word, printed out on paper and read using a finger to follow along, then read again backward from bottom to top.

 YOU COMPLETED YOUR RESUME! TIME FOR A GIFT.

Treat yourself to an evening out with friends. Take in a movie while enjoying food and drink at one of Portland's McMenamin's theaters or The Living Room Theater downtown.

SUPPLEMENTAL QUESTIONS

As of this writing, we've noticed that many local government, nonprofit, and educational organizations are asking applicants to answer supplemental questions as part of their application. In the case of government positions, the emerging trend is to replace the cover letter with supplemental questions. Many of the guidelines presented here also apply to supplemental questions—back up your answers with examples and achievements wherever possible.

You found a great job listing, you wrote a targeted resume, and now you need a cover letter. What exactly is a cover letter supposed to do—isn't it the same as the resume? Absolutely not!

A cover letter should complement your resume, not repeat it. It is a sales letter targeted to the specific position and employer. It is your chance to showcase your qualifications and accomplishments. It is also an opportunity to connect your skills and achievements with the requirements of the job posting and explain how related experiences from other employment or education transfer to meet the employer's needs. As with the resume, use achievements—quantifiable if you have them—to demonstrate your successes.

Now you may be wondering, "How should the cover letter look?" Of course, your chosen industry and the directions on the position announcement will influence what to include in your cover letter. There are, however, eleven basic content and design guidelines to follow.

1. **Length:** Most cover letters are one page.

2. **Visual Consistency:** Use the same header, footer, font, and design elements that are in your resume to create a visual brand that prospective employers will associate with your name. In the samples, notice how **Rebecca Recruited** and **Estelle Example** achieve a consistent look.

3. **Subject Line:** Identify the target position and any reference numbers.

4. **Salutation:** Address the letter to a person—if after thorough research this is not possible, consider using "Dear Hiring Manager" or eliminate the salutation. If eliminating the salutation, consider emphasizing the subject line or develop an attention-grabbing headline.

5. **The Hook:** Start your cover letter with a powerful sentence. Think "attention getter" similar to public speeches. Notice how eloquently **Ivan Illustration** pulls this off.

6. **Tone and Language:** Write with a professional, yet personable, tone. Use direct language that fits the culture of the organization. Avoid big words that you think make you sound smart. Research the vocabulary used on the company website and in the position announcement and integrate a similar tone into your writing style. Demonstrate enthusiasm for the position and employer.

7. **First Paragraph:** State the reason for your letter, include the job title, and where you learned about the job posting. If you know someone in the organization, by all means, please name drop. Introduce the main qualifications you have to offer.

8. **Second Paragraph:** In this paragraph, you have three options:
   A. For a nonprofit or mission-driven company, describe your understanding of their mission and your prior experience or commitments that align with their needs and goals.

STEER CLEAR OF THESE COMMON MISTAKES!

- *Do not use "Dear Sir/Madam" and "To Whom It May Concern." This is an outdated practice.*
- *Try to avoid starting too many sentences with I and My.*

OUR SAMPLE COVER LETTERS

We've provided several sample cover letters to illustrate the guidelines we present. As you view the samples, keep in mind it is best practice to write a cover letter that clearly shows you know your industry and have researched the organization. You may notice some variation among the samples in style and tone to address characteristics of a specific industry or the mission/culture of an organization.

B. Address your knowledge and prior experience with one of your top competitive strengths. Back it up with an example. Capture the employer's attention by sharing relevant skills, using keywords, and stating any major accomplishments.

C. Explain potential questions, such as gaps in employment or swerves in a career direction that may arise about your resume.

9. **Third and Fourth Paragraphs:** Reiterate and expand on one to three skills, accomplishments, or characteristics from your resume. Give examples with results. Demonstrate how related experiences transfer to meet the needs of the employer.

*Note: Some position announcements ask you to address each qualification specifically in the cover letter. In this case, make sure you use bold, bullets, or a format of your choice to emphasize each qualification and then address it with examples and achievements. **Melanie Mockup** uses bullets and bold to call attention to each qualification, followed by achievements that directly address them.*

10. **Closing Paragraph:** Reiterate the best way to contact you; recap what you can do for the organization; make a call to action—ask for the interview; indicate you will contact them to schedule a meeting; thank them for their time and consideration.

11. **Signature:** Close with "Sincerely"; be sure to sign above your name. If you are submitting your cover letter electronically, you can sign using a script font.

Tip

Start your cover letter with an attention-grabbing introductory sentence; make them want to read further!

Henry Hired

Wilsonville, Oregon | (503) 123-xxx67 | henryemailhere@gmail.com

September 6, 2017

Ric Recruiter
Senior Corporate Recruiter
HD Device USA

RE: Director of Consumer Survey

I am excited to be considered for Director of Consumer Survey at HD Device USA. I am impressed by the products and business solutions provided by HD, surely partly owed to your investment in market research and strategic analysis to drive product creation. I bring over 20 years of project management in both primary research (qualitative and quantitative) and secondary research (market intelligence and strategic analysis), helping grow success as a problem solver and visionary.

I am a skilled project manager who collaborates with vendors and teammates to generate quality information solutions on-time and within budget. I have done extensive research in the areas of segmentation, new product evaluation and testing, and product commercialization. The 200+ projects I managed resulted in identifying new business opportunities and supporting the development of new product and market solutions. In fact, some of this research has changed company approaches and strategy regarding organization structure, marketing processes, product positioning and targeting.

For example, as Senior Marketing Intelligence Manager at G Company, I let a team that redesigned everything from working with vendors to how data was collected, analyzed and used. By evaluating what wasn't working, I was able to guide an improved long-term data collections strategy to continually interact with target markets and collect relevant information. This restructuring effort improved data quality and reduced collection costs by up to 90% on some projects. I am impressed with the rate at which HD has introduced innovative products to the market, such as the Ultra Sports Ethernet port to improve connection speed. My efforts will ensure HD captures efficient performance measures to adapt to this quickly evolving market segment.

I'm also an innovative problem solver who thrives on helping and advising others. Decision-makers quickly see I understand their goals and view me as a credible resource because they are in roles I have held in the past. I also articulate difficult situations and solutions in a manner that is easy to understand and can be conveyed to various stakeholders. Clients value my innovative nature, particularly as it relates to the realities and constraints typically faced in developing processes, strategies and projects that generate winning solutions. I look forward to responding to the needs of HD's team from senior management in HD's corporate office in Boston to the Portland distribution center.

In summary, my project management skills and visionary problem-solving capabilities are what I can bring to HD as your new Director of Consumer Survey. I look forward to discussing skills and qualifications with you in person.

Sincerely,

Henry Hired

ESTELLE EXAMPLE

Forest Town, Oregon 97200 ∫ 000-123-4567 ∫ estelle.example@gmail.com

August 1, 2017

Mr. Adam Adamson
Pacific First Credit Union
1234 SW River Road
Forest Town, Oregon, 97000

RE: Human Resources Assistant

Dear Mr. Adamson:

Pacific First Credit Union needs a quality person to fill the open position of Human Resources Assistant, and I believe I am your solution. I bring over 15 years' experience providing reliable administrative support in a human resource environment, and I would like to bring my results-oriented skills to Pacific First Credit Union.

I am returning to a career in human resources to capitalize on my experience and education. I have a human resources certificate from Forest Town University, and I am finishing my final course for my associate degree in social science this summer. Delivering quality work and friendly service is the cornerstone of my values, and my dedication to both appear throughout my diverse career and administrative background.

In my current role, as a barista at Coffee Cup Time, I was recognized for providing superior customer service and communicating solutions to management. It is my desire to contribute my knowledge, experience, education, and training to support Pacific First Credit Union and their community.

I thrive in a team environment and successfully communicate and collaborate as a team member to achieve quality results and enjoy working on assignments independently. When working with others, they describe me as a team builder, sensitive to confidentiality needs, positive, dependable, organized, and diligent. These qualities are in direct alignment with the qualities you seek for the Human Resources Assistant position.

My resume is enclosed to provide you with details of my qualifications. It would be mutually beneficial for us to meet in-person and discuss how I can support Pacific First Credit Union. I will contact you in two weeks to explore the possibility of scheduling an appointment.

Thank you for your time and consideration.

Sincerely,

Estelle Example

Enclosure: Resume

Rebecca Recruited

PORTLAND, OR 97213 | REBECCAJRECRUITED@GMAIL.COM |503-123-4567

February 15, 2018

Robin Recruiter
Director of Recruiting
2100 SW Beautiful Parkway
Beautiful Town, OR 99933

Re: Project Coordinator

Dear Ms. Recruiter,

As a third-generation native of Washington and an Oregon transplant, I am excited about the possibility of joining We R Environment and Associates, a firm with deep roots on the west coast and a strong commitment to collaboration. I am passionate about the application of sustainable practices and appreciate your values of innovation and creativity and the emphasis on stewardship in your work.

I have over five years of combined experience in customer service, project coordination, and office management. Multiple employers and colleagues have praised my determination, organization, teamwork, and creativity. I noticed you are seeking an excellent written and verbal communicator: I have been told that my willingness to ask questions combined with my professional warmth and friendly attitude makes project work smoother and easier.

I am particularly excited about the Project Coordinator position because of my knowledge and passion for the world of infrastructure; a passion that was piqued by interacting with We R Consulting's utility clients and immersing myself in the vast energy infrastructure involved in We R's work. I would be delighted to use my project coordination skills to build and improve transportation infrastructure as part of the We R Environment and Associates team.

As the western U.S. becomes more developed and technology rapidly transforms individual and mass transportation, the work you do will have a more significant and complex role to play in the market. I am sure that We R Environment and Associates will continue to be among the major players in this industry. I welcome the opportunity to discuss further how I can contribute to your firm and assist in reaching your goals.

Best,

Rebecca Recruited

Ivan I. Illustration

Cypress, Oregon | 503-123-4567 | ivan.illustration@gmail.com

August 1, 2017

Ms. Shelly Adams
Career Network Services
sadams@careernetworkservices.com

RE: Procurement Associate Position   **Job Reference #: 789-00-4567**

Dear Ms. Adams:

I have had a swoosh on my feet as-long-as I can remember. When I saw the position announcement for the Procurement Associate at Nike on the Career Network Services website, I made submitting application materials my priority.

If you ask me to accomplish a goal—I will. Utilizing over 12 years of experience in customer service, athletics, and professional management I bring problem-solving capabilities; the ability to develop organizational and communication strategies; and an achievement-focused style that will help Nike reach its long-term procurement goals.

Being self-directed and results-driven has been a true asset in accomplishing desired outcomes in demanding, fast-paced, and team-oriented environments. Building relationships with key internal and external stakeholders significantly contributed to ongoing success.

As an athlete and coach, I understand processes and how they relate to performance. This understanding directly corresponds to contributing to the supply chain process to source materials enabling Nike to continue to create the quality products people trust.

Taking the initiative results in success. When I joined Top Performing Athletics, the team was unknown and had no marketing or brand presence. Being a problem-solver, I took the initiative to design a crest to represent the group and set up team social media profiles to increase public awareness and event attendance. The results were hundreds of new fans, and achieving the goal of the U.S. Track and Field Olympic Trials—the crest is still worn by athletes during high profile competitions.

Whether on the track or in business, I am committed to achieving high-caliber performance just like Nike. For this reason, I look forward to meeting with you to discuss how I can help Nike reach its goals. It is easiest to reach me at 503-123-4567 or ivan.illustration@gmail.com.

Thank you for your time and consideration.

Sincerely,

Ivan I. Illustration

Enclosure: Resume

Melanie M. Mockup

Maplewood, Oregon 97000 | 503-123-4567 | m.mockup@gmail.com

"I am the kind of person you hire to improve processes." ~ Melanie Mockup

August 1, 2017

Ms. North West, Executive Director
Community Clinic of Poplar Oregon
1234 SE First Avenue
Poplar, Oregon 97000

"Melanie has impressed me with her unique ability to get efficiency and quality working in synthesis. She demonstrates a breadth of knowledge, experience, and support that serves our patients and co-workers. I believe Melanie's efforts led us to achieving more with our service." ~ Medical Director

RE: Program Manager

Dear Ms. West:

I share in the Community Clinic of Poplar's passion for creating access to quality care for all people. Managing and coordinating clinical operations for the past 13 years, I have worked in multiple capacities providing leadership, supervision, and cultivating relationships with patients, peers, and all levels of medical staff. Taking pride in always doing the best work possible has earned me a reputation as the go-to person who will go above and beyond to ensure quality patient care and create a cohesive team-oriented work environment. I would bring these qualities and the following:

- **Program and project management.** Demonstrated by an ongoing dedication to continuous quality improvement that increases program and process efficiency in a fast-paced continually changing medical setting. I took the initiative to develop new clinical review processes that solved scheduling and resource conflicts at Kaiser.

- **Leadership and training.** Acknowledged as a team leader who exemplifies collaboration at Kaiser, I strive to be present, improve productivity, and support patients and co-workers. As part of the new clinical review process, I developed curriculum and taught staff how to navigate the changes. Part of the process was ensuring availability at any time to assist with questions.

- **Relationship building.** Created and maintained trusting relationships essential to providing top quality customer service and patient care. Described by peers and patients as friendly, helpful, and knowledgeable.

- **Budget management.** Negotiated needed funds and conservatively managed monthly budgets for program operations at Home Living Center. Developed realistic projections with clear planning and thorough research.

- **Data analysis.** Developed a system to ensure a clear understanding of multiple types of data analysis. In my first supervisory position, I oversaw staff and collected data to ensure genetic integrity of new plant breeds to apply for agricultural patents. Additionally, while at Midland Rehabilitation, I tracked daily patient behavior activities to set up the individualized daily quality of life living programs.

Since this correspondence and the enclosed résumé can only provide you with a brief overview of my skills and accomplishments, I would welcome the opportunity to talk to you in person about how I can help the Community Clinic of Poplar continue to provide compassionate care to the community. My dedication to continuous improvement and open, team-oriented communication style would be an asset to your team. It is best to contact me at 503-123-4567 or m.mockup@gmail.com. Thank you for your consideration. I look forward to speaking with you soon.

Sincerely,

Melanie M. Mockup

Enclosure: Résumé

Connie Contributor Portland, OR | 503-123-4567 | conniesemailgoeshere@gmail.com

Jan 15, 2017

Heartfelt Non-Profit
000 SW 1st Ave
Portland, OR. 99999

Re: Development Associate

To Heartfelt Non-Profit,

I was delighted to read your current posting for a Development Associate. I am excited about the possibility of joining a team that contributed 18 million dollars in 2016 to meet the urgent needs of 8 million refugees. Please find my resume attached, and let me add a few details here on what I can bring to the Heartfelt's mission.

I have fourteen years combined experience in fundraising, telephone counseling, marketing and telephone-based sales. In the course of this I've been told I'm an excellent listener, quick to establish rapport, and have a warmly professional demeanor. A vice president emphasized how effective and appealing I was on the telephone.

One person I successfully cultivated over years remarked, "You always remember the last thing we talked about!" (Of course, I had documented our chats and then reviewed those notes right before my next contact with her.) I have spent most of my work life giving personalized attention, discerning where interest and passion lie, and taking sensible next steps to make good things happen. I am comfortable in asking people to do things, such as increasing their commitment. I am unalarmed at being told 'no'.

I'm a self-starter who also loves being part of a team. One supervisor told me I was unusually good at receiving feedback from her. Two others told me that coworkers found me an especially positive and encouraging presence. I have high standards for both the results I achieve and the relationship-building process I use to get there.

As a lifelong donor to humanitarian organizations, I am credible and sincere in conversations about giving. My interest in international aid and development is reflected in my husband's and my giving history, which includes Heartfelt's, Women to Women International and microloan programs in Rwanda and South America. I like the respectful way that Heartfelt treats its donors, and I especially like the way it respects communities in need by working with them on the agendas that they themselves set.

I'll respect your valuable time by keeping this letter brief. I hope to interview with you soon to discuss how I could be of service to your mission.

Sincerely,

Connie Contributor

Written by Vicki Lind and Kristin Schuchman

ZACHARY ZIGZAG   PORTLAND, OR ~ CELL: 555-123-4567 ~ EMAILGOESHERE@GMAIL.COM

June 1, 2017

William Willhire
Trust for Public Land
806 SW BusyStreet # 000
Portland, OR 99999

Re: Project Associate

Dear Mr. Willhire:

After meeting with Mike Manager to learn more about the Trust for Public Land's work, I am excited to submit my application for the position of Project Associate at Oregon Field Office. For the past seven years, I have broadly explored environmental issues and gained experience shaping environmental policy in government, journalism, and academic settings. Last year, I gave serious consideration to my career goal for the next ten years and decided to build on my environmental foundation to focus on a career in conservation.

In pursuit of this goal I am currently applying my research skills and policy expertise as a volunteer assistant to the government relation's staff at The Nature Conservancy. My specific tasks of researching sites, engaging property owners and other stakeholders, and preparing maps and informational material, have much in common with the Project Associate's duties at TPL.

I pursued my interest in making cities more livable as a research analyst at the Office of Sustainable Development (OSD). At OSD, I juggled multiple projects entailing research, project support, and coordination. My principal tasks included devising a blueprint for a policy and research division, through which OSD could influence the city's sustainability agenda by conceiving, independently funding, and partnering with the private sector to carry out demonstration projects. I balanced research and administrative support tasks to move projects forward.

I am firmly rooted in Oregon and familiar with its geography, politics, and culture. I care deeply about protecting its open spaces and can think of no organization so aligned with my goals as the Trust for Public Land. I admire TPL's tight focus on a pragmatic mission – to put high quality land in public ownership – and its entrepreneurial style. I'm especially drawn to TPL's vision of conserving land for people, from pristine ecosystems to urban brownfields.

As my resume indicates, I took a detour from my work in sustainability to pursue a doctorate in environmental history. After weighing the rewards of historical research against my desire to make a tangible contribution to the health of the environment, I packed up my research and analytical skills and brought them home to Oregon, with a newly clarified focus and the hopes of finding an entry position in a conservation organization. I'm confident that I've found the right position as Project Associate at TPL.

Sincerely,

Zachary Zigzag

Catherine Creative

Portland OR 97203 | 415.518.6660 | catherine.emailgoeshere@gmail.com

March 5, 2017

Attn: Funnelbox
Re: Creative Director Position

Dear Funnelbox:

Your job posting for Creative Director immediately grabbed my attention. I like the tone and energy of the post and am very interested in a company and position that inspires passion, encourages knowledge and growth, and maintains a sense of humor. Your sizzle reel has an amazing sense of kinetics and and an inspiring scope of work. One of my favorite vignettes is the "Klinkle" piece. I'm completely blown away by the story and editing, and the trend of effective and seamless visual effects into video marketing is of particular interest to me.

For me, my work is my passion and an integral part of my life. Every day it influences how I experience the world. I have spent my entire career as a Lighting Technical Director and Artist in visual effects for major films, at companies where we worked hard but reveled in the fact that at the end of the day our work incites spark and engagement in the viewing public. I feel my showreel is a great indicator of the scope of my work:

https://vimeo.com/205255108
password: mypassword123

As a person who enjoys collaboration and new and unique challenges more than anything I believe I would be a great fit for your team. At Lucasfilm I was consistently promoted into leadership roles and assigned the most challenging work because of my abiding interest in expanding my creative boundaries and willingness to step outside my comfort zone. I would be thrilled to have a chance to discuss the Creative Director position with you.

Sincerely,

Catherine Creative

"I do believe in the old saying, "What does not kill you makes you stronger." Our experiences, good and bad, make us who we are. By overcoming difficulties, we gain strength and maturity." —Angelina Jolie

HOLD ON TO YOUR OPTIMISM AND RESILIENCE

In this section, we've explained the latest trends in resume/cover letter writing and have helped you clarify your options and organize your steps. If you are still having trouble getting started, it may help to imagine us sitting here, observing your doubts and reluctance...acting as calm guides to get you moving. We are here to remind you it is natural to feel anxious when putting your best professional self out there. We are big believers in chunking overwhelming tasks into 20-minute time blocks with limited step-by-step goals—and be sure to give yourself regular stretch or tea breaks as you work.

OVERCOMING DISCOURAGING NEWS

As you absorb what it will take to get through the screening process in HR, your reaction is likely to be, "Holy Cow! It will take me a long time to tailor each resume." That is true; it will take a long time—we estimate four to six hours for each resume and cover letter. The good news is you can reduce that time by developing a system to save and repurpose your content. Save and label each resume, and you will soon have a bank of accomplishment statements to match to a variety of job announcements.

Let go of the outdated belief that success is related to the number of resumes you send out. It is more reasonable to set a goal of sending out one high-quality tailored resume every week or two for positions for which you are well qualified. As you do a closer analysis of position requirements, you will discard more announcements whenever your skills do not match the first four or five minimum qualifications (unless you have an inside connection who can recommend that a hiring manager look at your resume).

"Don't fear failure: the only time you must not fail is the last time you try." —Phil Knight

When our clients pick jobs that are a good match and follow our advice for tailoring, they are receiving at least one call back for every four resumes they send.

BOUNCING BACK FROM REJECTION

When you find a job you really want and put considerable effort into tailoring a resume and cover letter, it is exciting when you push the "Send" button. Your sense of hope, however, may sag when days creep by and you haven't received a call for an interview. Currently, most employers do not send resume receipt notifications, and they actively discourage phone calls. If you get through the screening and give a strong interview, it is natural that your hope will soar. So, it is particularly painful to receive a rejection when you expected a win.

Being able to bounce back from rejection is key to sanity and success. It is crucial you realize that a rejection from a future employer is not a rejection of you as a valuable human being. Instead, it is a statement that another individual has skills, expertise, and characteristics that are a better fit according to the employer's needs.

Naturally, you will be disappointed. Give yourself permission to take a break and spend a few days on the couch, in the woods, or reading a mystery novel. If this doesn't get you into action, you might consider a rigorous exercise regimen, or watch an inspiring movie in which the hero, heroine, or team overcome serious odds. If none of these suggestions work, it may be time to invest in a professional. This person could be a job search coach or a resume writer who knows the secrets to get through the automated tracking software system and the interview process. If lassitude or anxiety set in and block you from forward momentum, you might want to consider seeing a counselor to strengthen your coping skills and reenergize your job search process.

Tip

Keeping the faith can be particularly difficult after you've had an interview you thought went well but didn't result in an offer. We recommend reading this article after each interview to remind you to stay hopeful and optimistic. In fact, you might want to bookmark this article, so it is handy at any time in your job search when you need some reassuring words and an extra boost of motivation.

Step 4
Find Your Networking Style

"Networking is not all fattening appetizers and bad Chardonnay. Find what works for you."
—Kathryn Minshew, founder and CEO of The Muse, a career development and job search site

"We can't help everyone, but everyone can help someone." —Ronald Reagan

As mentioned previously in this handbook, networking is a vital part of a successful job search strategy. Experts say that 50–80 percent of all positions are obtained by networking. Vicki did an informal study and reviewed the records of successful clients who have worked with her over the past several years. True to expectations, networking played a role in 60–70 percent of the success stories.

We found that the role of networking was quite diverse. Contacts helped our clients by:

- Forwarding job announcements that otherwise would have been missed.

- Creating a new position based on valuable contributions made during volunteering.

- Putting in a good word to the hiring manager or search committee.

- Providing inside information about what to emphasize on the resume and during the interview.

- Making introductions to key decision-makers to learn about their challenges and/or upcoming openings.

"Should networking be part of my job search?" is not the right question. The useful question is, "How much and what type of networking is a match for my schedule, personality, and engagement with LinkedIn?" In this section, we help you answer those questions.

Networking to Match Your Personality diffuses any notions that networking means going to a myriad of events where you need to schmooze to promote yourself. That is only a fit for extroverts who are stimulated by dynamic crowds. If you are an introvert, effective networking may be having tea with a few people whom you enjoy who are eager to help you. In this article, we introduce you to extroverts and introverts who used different networking strategies to show you the variety of options.

We've provided a ***Network Contact List*** for you to write down the names of past colleagues, friends, and relatives who could offer help. Of course, if you prefer using your phone, tablet, or computer, you can capture those names and their contact information on your device.

As we've mentioned before, we highly encourage you to use LinkedIn. You may be thinking, "Ugh, do I have to? I really don't want to bother with it." In ***Network with LinkedIn*** we make a case for this powerful tool and address any reservations and barriers you might have to using LinkedIn as part of your networking strategy.

In ***LinkedIn: Create an Effective Profile*** we help you craft a profile that includes an attention-getting headline, summary, photo, and work history that will attract employers looking for someone just like you. Then we move on to ***LinkedIn: Build Your Network*** to show you how to connect with friends, family, school alumni, and professional colleagues to build a basic network of contacts.

In ***LinkedIn: Expand and Tap Your Network*** we describe how to expand your connections by tapping folks who are contacts of your contacts. We also encourage you to reach out to these extended contacts for job leads or informational interviews.

NETWORKING TO MATCH YOUR PERSONALITY

Traditional models of networking were based on a hierarchical system in which job seekers aimed to meet people higher up the organizational ladder. While meeting leaders is still important, we prefer a more community-minded approach.

When we see ourselves as part of a web—like Charlotte's iconic web—we are all interconnected in multiple directions around a common center. In Charlotte's case, the spider spun the words *some pig* in the center of her web. Imagine that Charlotte has woven a phrase in the middle of your job-search web that captures your ideal job. A technical writer in health care might select *life-saving words* or a person in recycling might imagine *garbage reduction*. The spokes radiating out from this core represent the people and organizations that connect with this central concern. The purpose of your networking is to meet as many people as possible with whom you share this core passion in order to exchange ideas and leads.

NETWORKING FOR INTROVERTS

Magazines and internet sites abound with articles that have titles like *Five Easy Steps to Networking or Schmooze or Lose*. Too many of these articles are written by extroverts who assume that introverts can (and want to) mimic their style. The word "schmooze" connotes getting to know someone expressly to advance your agenda—which is probably incongruent with the value that introverts place on deep, authentic relationships.

The following techniques were used by introverted clients who applied only what was consistent with their natural proclivity to engage in substantive conversations with people who share their professional interests. These interactions can be in person over tea, or over the internet through LinkedIn or other social media. As you review these examples, envision which ones might be pleasant for you to try.

Local Examples:

Many years ago, **Vicki** decided she needed a half-time job with benefits to complement her new private practice as a career counselor. Although she can be outgoing in familiar settings, she has a strong preference to spend free time at home or with a few close friends. She kept avoiding what she thought at that time was required for effective networking—going out to varied activities to meet many new people. Finally, she decided to honor her own style and invite eight of her close colleagues to lunch to form an ad hoc "advisory board." In advance, she reminded them of her top skills and asked them to provide her with the names of organizations and specific people to contact. This brainstorming session generated about 15 leads, including the name of a dean at PCC Rock Creek who hired her as a career specialist for the summer, followed by a contact at ProtoCall Services where she was hired for a part-time position on a mental health crisis line.

- **Marcy**, an introvert, came to Portland because of her husband's job and didn't have a local network of friends or colleagues. Her gift—and the motivating force—behind her successful networking was her natural curiosity and her passion for mapmaking (GIS) and protecting natural resources, especially water. She used self-talk and the support of members in her job support group to motivate her to attend Green Drinks. She promised her support group she would talk to at least two people she didn't know at Green Drinks as well as add some people to her LinkedIn network.

When she got to Green Drinks, she took a deep breath and said to herself, "If I'm only going to meet one or two people, I might as well meet someone who is well-connected in Portland's green community." She introduced herself to Will, who cofacilitated Green Drinks and had 1,000 contacts on his LinkedIn site. Once Marcy was engaged in a one-on-one conversation with the ever-friendly Will, she no longer needed deep breathing or self-talk because she had found the meaningful one-on-one conversations that are safe and comfortable for introverts. She enjoyed reporting back to her support group that she had followed through on her intentions.

- **Patricia** wanted a position that used her strengths in analyzing and organizing data and writing complex reports in service of sustainability. She hoped others would keep their eyes open for position announcements that matched her skill set. As an introvert, however, she did not have a large network. She was reluctant to contact the people she had met and initiate the requisite small talk. Instead, she signed up to organize the poster display booths for a large environmental conference. Her role was to contact each environmental organization to coordinate the details of their display.

She left this strategic volunteer activity on a first-name basis with key players in her desired field. A strong writer, she periodically sent updates to this group via email and reminded them of her job search goal. When an appropriate project opened up at Metro, three people saw the match and forwarded the notice to Patricia, who successfully landed the position. And, best of all, she avoided loosely structured chitchat.

NETWORKING FOR EXTROVERTS

One of the defining characteristics of an extrovert is they enjoy meeting new people, which makes networking easier for them. Picture Bill Clinton's face and how it seems to genuinely light up when he meets strangers. It's been written that he started a Rolodex (a circular holder for business cards that physically sits on a desk) of contacts his first year of college. He never stopped collecting cards, and his database became one of his most enviable tools. Of course, he had zero compunction about asking everyone on the list for exactly what he wants.

Local Examples:

- An extrovert, **Macy**, adopted the following advice offered by Marty Nemko, author of *Cool Careers for Dummies*. "Call 100, yes 100 people who like you—everyone from your parents' best friend to your ex-lover, from your old professor to your new haircutter."

- **Sam** was a lawyer with a consulting firm that had a lot of public sector clients. He found a job posting for an executive director position with the Oregon Community Foundation. The challenge was to get past the human resources screening since he did not meet the second major requirement: five years' experience in a leadership role at a nonprofit. Sam had a well-developed LinkedIn network and he looked up the name of the hiring manager as well as several board members who were likely to be part of the hiring process. He found that one of his past coworkers, a great fan of his work, was a 1st-degree connection with the hiring manager and one of his public sector clients knew another manager. He messaged them saying, "I see you are connected to X. I am very enthusiastic about being an excellent match for the position of Y, even though I do not technically meet one of the requirements. Can you put in a good word for me?" Both his connections responded right away with an offer to call or message their contacts, and rave about what Sam could bring to OCF. He won the interview!

- **Jessica**, Vicki's eldest daughter, is naturally social (a born extrovert) and stays in touch with an enormous network of friends and former colleagues through Facebook and LinkedIn. She eagerly goes out of her way to help people in her networking circles and seldom loses contact with old boyfriends, bosses, neighbors, and college mates. People in her Gen-X clan (as well as younger people) know they are always on call for one another and social media is the central connecting hub.

Jessica has obtained two major jobs through this network. First, she wanted to use her creative and writing skills for an organization devoted to women's issues. She targeted a few ideal organizations and emailed her network to see who knew whom. A friend of a friend, whom she had met at a party, worked for Oxygen (Oprah's now-defunct women's website). Jessica's contact put in a good word for her which led to her getting an interview. Once again, she drew on her network to research the people who would interview her so that she would connect well with each of them. As a result, she was hired as the producer for Thrive, Oxygen's online health site for women.

- **Alicia**, another extrovert with a huge smile and idealism to match, volunteered to staff a recycling-program booth at Portland's Home and Garden Show. She introduced herself to some people who worked for the City of Portland's Bureau of Planning and Sustainability. During lively conversations with them, she asked about opportunities at the bureau. The following month a position opened and she applied. She was not just a name in the huge stack of applicants; she was the applicant with the energetic personal style. Alicia was asked to interview, and then landed the job as a multifamily specialist.

Getting started with networking can be difficult so we urge the shy and reluctant among you—as well as the vivacious and outgoing—to make a starter list of activities, groups, and people who could boost your job search, Then, get active on LinkedIn, attend events, and participate in activities...you'll find yourself networking in no time!

GIVE YOURSELF A GIFT TO ENERGIZE YOU

Introverts and extroverts refuel their tanks in different ways. If you're an introvert, take some "alone" time--read a book, play a video game, or take a bath. If you're an extravert, spend time with friends--go out for happy hour, host a party, or hit the dance floor at the Crystal Ballroom's 80's video dance attack on Friday nights.

List 20 people you could call, email and/or meet for coffee to network. Select people whom you could ask about job leads and/or contacts they may know inside of your targeted organizations.

Date	Name	Phone	Email	Notes

The ideal candidate is someone who shares your desired job title or industry. However, networking is based on the idea that your friend or colleague may have a spouse, sibling, or neighbor who can help you in your job search. Remember Roy D. Chapin, Jr.'s aphorism: "Luck is the time when preparation and opportunity meet."

If you are hesitant to contact people you do not know very well or have not seen for a while, begin with people you enjoy and with whom you feel comfortable. Even if they do not have a lead, you will enjoy the conversation. Consider reaching out to your relatives, neighbors, old classmates, past coworkers, people you have met at seminars or with whom you do business, etc. Err on the side of inclusiveness.

You may want to:

- Ask your two best friends to give you more leads.

- Go to an event or professional meeting in your field.

- Ask your career services professional, if you are working with one, for additional names.

- Check with your alumni association for names of local people in your desired profession.

Tip

Don't forget about LinkedIn. Select one of your contacts who is well-connected and may want to be of help. Review their connections and open the profiles of people who interest you. If you want your connection to introduce you, send them a message asking if they are willing to make the introduction. In the remaining articles in this section we show you how to get going on LinkedIn.

NETWORK WITH LINKEDIN

Given that LinkedIn is the world's largest professional network with 500 million users, there is no denying that having a LinkedIn presence can boost your job search strategy. Though not everyone is cut out to be a LinkedIn power user, every professional should have what we call the LinkedIn "job search starter duo": A **profile** to be seen by prospective employers and a **network** of at least fifty people—usually present or past colleagues, alumni, or friends. These folks can help you expand your network by introducing—or **connecting**—you to others. Many potential employers expect to be able to find you on LinkedIn to get a quick electronic overview of who you are as a professional.

Once you have a profile and a network, you might decide to move beyond the basic activities. Vicki thought she would be a lightweight on LinkedIn, using it only to contact and get current with old colleagues and alumni. She was surprised to discover she enjoyed finding people on LinkedIn after networking events and expanding her network by reaching out to them to connect. It's a kind of newfangled village where people help each other forage for valuable jobs and career boosts.

LINKEDIN CAN HELP YOU LAND A JOB

Here's a sampling of the many ways that our clients have used LinkedIn to land jobs:

- **Bev H.**, a project manager in waste reduction, sent individual messages through LinkedIn to 15 colleagues in her network. One of them sent her a position announcement that was a perfect match.

- **Jim S.**, a training director, loaded his LinkedIn profile with keywords in his desired field. A recruiter from Providence found his profile and invited him in for an interview.

- **Marianne H.**, a senior-level HR manager, applied for a VP-level position in a large nonprofit. She asked her LinkedIn contacts who were connected to the hiring manager to put in a good word for her with the board. She landed the interview.

- **George F.**, a UX/graphic designer identified midsized creative agencies through LinkedIn's company pages and built relationships with creatives who work there. One of them forwarded a link to the creative director when a position opened up.

- **Drew G.** wanted a position with the State of Oregon. While his networking efforts with employees in targeted departments did not help him meet hiring managers in this tightly regimented hiring environment, his LinkedIn contacts did apprise him of the complex process used by the state, and how to accrue maximum points on his applications, resumes, and supplemental questions.

ADDRESS YOUR RESERVATIONS

You may have reservations about using LinkedIn, especially if you're new to using social media for a job search. Once you understand how to find individuals on LinkedIn who can answer your questions, these reservations will likely fade away.

If you are still hesitant, we address the four common barriers to using LinkedIn here:

1. **You dislike or distrust social media:** Maybe you're an introvert, inexperienced with social media, or have had a bad experience on social media. LinkedIn has some safeguards built in because you control what is posted on your site and whom you're connected to, and you can disconnect from someone without them ever knowing. None of our clients has ever had a bad experience on LinkedIn.

2. LinkedIn may seem somewhat conventional and a bit chilly: It's true that it's not as fun and playful as Facebook or Instagram, which may bother you if you are creative or a free spirit. Dig a little deeper and you'll see that people's photos and branding are not one-size-fits-all. You'll find that people in creative and casual fields actually play a bit with their overall presentation. For example, some dog companions and kooky facial expressions appear in profile photos or backgrounds of folks in nonconventional companies.

3. You're not technical: Don't think of LinkedIn as a technology tool. Rather, think of it as today's phone book, but with a focus on each person's professional background and skills presented in a consistent and easy-to-access format.

4. Your current employer will see that you're exploring new job opportunities: It used to be true that folks actively used LinkedIn when they were looking for new jobs. Today, it has become the hub of all professional communication. In fact, 40 percent of LinkedIn members use it daily to stay in touch with their network. There's no reason to connect with your current employer on LinkedIn if you don't want them to know you are looking for a new job. If you are already connected, it's easy to disconnect from them and they'll never know!

If you fear that updating your current profile will alert current employers of your itch to move on, there is a **Share Profile Edits** switch that you can set to **No** to ensure that your updates are not shared with your LinkedIn community. When you are ready to reveal your changes, you can set this switch to **Yes**. To make sure this switch defaults to **No**, go into the **Settings & Privacy** section in your account, click on **Privacy**, and set this switch to **No**.

We hope that we have alleviated any reservations you might have had to using LinkedIn. Given that it is such a powerful tool, we hope you will at least give it a try. In the following articles, we will help you do just that by guiding you through the steps to create a profile and build and expand on your network.

Tip

If you have any concerns about privacy, we recommend exploring these two LinkedIn features: The Settings & Privacy option that occurs when you click on Me under your profile photo, and the Edit My Public Profile and URL setting to the right of your profile page. For more details on these features, refer to the LinkedIn help system.

LINKEDIN: CREATE AN EFFECTIVE PROFILE

Part of launching a robust job search is having an effective LinkedIn profile that articulates what you are seeking and what you have to offer.

These seven components comprise the elements of your LinkedIn profile:

1. NAME

If you have an advanced degree or certification, include the initials after your last name. For example, "Cynthia Dettman JD, MSW" is pretty darn impressive because the JD quickly connotes a sharp analytical mind, and the MSW a sympathetic ear.

2. HEADLINE

The 122 characters of your headline are seen first and therefore this is your most important real estate. Historically, your most recent position title was always your headline, but now there are more choices. If you are unemployed or pivoting in a new direction, you want to replace your job title (or add to it) with keywords and competencies you want to use on your next job.

Note: You can keep your job title without additional keywords only if it is impressive and reflects the type of position that you are seeking.

Consider the keywords specific to your industry a hiring manager or someone in HR would type in the search box if they were looking to fill a position you want. You can get ideas for keywords by looking at job announcements or reviewing the LinkedIn profiles of people who hold the job titles you are seeking.

The following examples include job titles while others focus exclusively on competitive skills or expertise:

- Director of Public Relations and Marketing | Expert at raising brand awareness and developing partnerships

- Speech Pathologist giving voice to children with Asperger's Syndrome

- VP of Sales | Experience growing and leading global teams of 100+

- Social Media Expert driving successful B2B and B2C campaigns on a shoestring budget

- Graphic Designer able to give life to dry facts with stunning infographics

- Environmental Policy Analyst and SQL Expert seeking opportunities

- Six Sigma Master Black Belt dedicated to process excellence in email operations

3. PHOTO

Whether you decide on a professional photo or want to tap a family member adept with an iPhone, your photo's style depends on your profession. Portland has a lot of subcultures—from grassroots nonprofits to traditional global corporations. So, some photos are edgy while others still require donning a tailored suit.

All photos should show you with a smile and:

- Be at least 200px by 200px. We recommend using a larger one (400px by 400px) but with a 1x1 aspect ratio and then reducing its size.

- Have a neutral, solid-colored, or simple background which keeps the focus on you.

- Have an image that isn't too busy (especially if your background has images in it like trees or leaves) and is relevant to your field. For example, only include children and dogs if you work with them.

Tip

The free version of LinkedIn will get you started. You do not need to pay for the whistles and bells of LinkedIn Premium to have a decent profile.

Professional Photos

LinkedIn claims that a professional photo increases the chances your profile will be viewed. We agree that a sharp, professional photo is often worth the cost.

- Pick a photographer willing to take several shots with different expressions and a mix of poses both facing and looking away from the camera. You can use the additional photos for other professional needs.

- Ask the photographer to work with different lighting and focus techniques.

- Creative industries like advertising usually respond better to photos with a well-done casual feel and a bit of flair. Think about asking your photographer about black-and-white, an interesting background, or an unusual angle.

DIY Photos

If you plan on tapping a friend or family photographer, select some samples for them to emulate. LinkedIn includes a basic photo editor so you can make simple touch-ups.

Here are examples of how two clients approached their outdoor DIY photo choices:

- **Colleen Kaleda** worked in development in Africa, so her photo was taken in an Ethiopian village.

- **Ray Hurt** came to Portland from Macy's Corporate Headquarters in San Francisco and had a stiff professional photo, which he promptly switched out for one with a casual Portland outdoors look. Because Nike and Adidas were his target employers, he showed a little more of his clothing—a contemporary casual jacket.

4. SUMMARY

The Summary section is the most important section of your overall profile after the headline and photo. It is particularly critical if your most recent job experience does not showcase the skills that are most relevant to the job you want. Keep it short and punchy because only three lines of your copy will show without an additional click to "show more."

- **Example 1:** Here is a strong example that summarizes experience and includes both skills (researching, program strategies) and industry keywords (renewable energy, greenhouse gas).
  With eleven years of experience, I possess a proven record of researching, designing, and implementing innovative marketing and program strategies for renewable energy and greenhouse gas mitigation. Strengthened by customer insights, these strategies result in measurable energy and emissions reduction.

- **Example 2:** This teacher has selected the highlights from her career including a result (raised reading state test scores).
  Highly qualified English and humanities classroom teacher skilled in working with both high-achieving and low-performing students. Developed model high school literacy coaching program and school-wide reading strategies resulting in raised reading state test scores.

5. EXPERIENCE

This section is quite simple; you can cull part of the copy from your resume but not all of it. List your duties and major accomplishments in short paragraphs (no more than four lines) or bullet points (no more than six) focusing on measurable results and with an eye to maximizing its punch.

6. RECOMMENDATIONS

We live in a networked world in which relationships and reputations matter. LinkedIn recommendations validate your reputation based on comments from people who have seen your work in action.

In today's legal climate, most companies are hesitant to give full recommendations for past employees. When a previous manager or colleague is contacted at work for a reference, they commonly refer the caller to HR, who only shares the dates of employment and if you are eligible for rehire. Therefore, employers are increasingly relying on LinkedIn recommendations as well as reference checks. Since you get to choose and review the comments from these recommendations, you run no risk of being blindsided by a bad reference.

Here are a few pointers from Patricia Pickett (balancecareers.com) on how to ask for a recommendation:

- **Use the LinkedIn Recommendations Tool**
  Access the recommendations tool from your Profile page. The first way is from the drop-down menu next to your profile picture. Select the **Ask to be recommended** option. This takes you to a page where you manage the recommendations you give and receive.

  You'll be prompted for the position you want to be recommended for and from whom you want the recommendation. Choose up to three people at a time.

- **Send Personalized Messages or Emails**
  You might want to email your contact to see if it's okay to request a recommendation using LinkedIn's recommendation option. If you have a strong connection with the person and you know they'd be happy to give you a good recommendation, send them a personalized message from within LinkedIn with your request.

- **Write a Recommendation for Someone First**
  Write a recommendation for someone if you can attest to their professional skills, knowledge, and characteristics. If you're shy about asking a contact for a recommendation, take the initiative and write a recommendation for them first, without their knowledge. Your connection will be notified, providing them an incentive to return the favor. Writing recommendations for others can serve to remind you that this kind of support can be pleasurable rather than a burden, making it easier for you to request recommendations in return.

- **Contact People You Know Well**
  The recommendations of past managers or clients have the most clout. Past colleagues with solid job titles are also valid sources. Connections who have not had a close working relationship with you can't offer concrete, honest feedback about you as a professional.

- **Word Your Request Politely**
  When you ask for a recommendation, make it clear that the recipient isn't under any obligation. Use phrases like if *it's not too much trouble* or *when you have a chance*. This communicates that you respect their time, and you recognize they are doing you a favor.

- **Provide Content Suggestions**
  Most times, people are eager to write recommendations and are open to guidance. You might offer several skills and attributes they could choose to write about. You don't have to feed your contacts every word. Remind them of your individual and team successes and they'll usually vouch for you. Here's an example:
  "If it's not too much trouble, could you provide some comments on my performance during the XYZ contract that finished ahead of time and under budget?"

7. INTERESTS

Your interests are comprised of people and organizations you follow in four categories:

- Schools you attended

- Past and present employers/companies

- Groups, which provide a way to interact with others who work in your field or target company

- Influencers

Now is a good time to select a few **influencers** relevant to your field. The difference between following an influencer and a connection is that you do not expect influencers to engage with you and help you in your search. Top influencers like Bill Gates and Ariana Huffington are a tad busy with other matters to concern themselves with your job search.

When someone views your profile, the influencers you follow tell them which thought leaders shape your thinking. It gives them another lens on what you care about, and a possible commonality around which to engage. It can be fun to think of leaders who move and motivate you professionally. For example, Vicki started following Adam Grant after she heard him on Podcasts talking about how we can find motivation and meaning, build productive and supportive cultures, and lead more generous and creative lives.

UPDATE, PAUSE, REPEAT

After you have updated your profile, ask a career professional, friend, or colleague to look at it. Give them a heads up about the type of employer who will be viewing your profile and what you want to convey. Then, ask them honestly:

- Does my photo and headline present the image that I want?

- Are there any typos or grammatical errors?

- Are my strengths and accomplishments presented loud and clear?

- And, by the way, do you have connections with whom I should connect?

Think of your profile as an ever-changing, ever-evolving snippet about your professional life. You don't have to get it right all in one sitting and it will change as your professional needs and wants change. Work on it until your "brain is full." Then, pick it up again to complete more steps until you are proud of the final result.

LINKEDIN: BUILD YOUR NETWORK

Your LinkedIn network is like having your own directory of people who are rooting for your career success and would be glad to help you achieve your goals. Begin by adding friends, colleagues, and professional acquaintances to your network so that you can keep in touch (even if their email or phone number changes) and stay informed about their professional moves.

FIND PEOPLE YOU KNOW AND INVITE THEM TO CONNECT

There are five ways to help you find people you know:

1. You can select **the high school and colleges you attended**, along with the year you graduated. You'll see a list of people from your graduating class who are on LinkedIn.

2. You can **enter your past employer** in the search box to generate a list of profiles of people who work for that employer.

3. LinkedIn will review **your email address book** (Outlook, Gmail, etc.) and tell you who is also on LinkedIn.

4. When you click on **My Network**, LinkedIn will offer suggestions of **people you may know** and want to invite to join your network.

5. If you already know the name of someone you would like to add to your network, simply enter their name in the search field to view their profile.

Once you find people, decide if you want to invite them to connect, because you want to stay in touch and/or because they work in a field of interest to you. We recommend that you include friends as well as professional contacts. Even if the person is not in your profession, they may have someone in their network who can be of help. If you remember their name and face, invite them into your network unless, of course, you have had a negative interaction with them in the past.

WORDING YOUR INVITATIONS

When you invite someone from your past to connect, it's important to write a personalized message rather than the cold standard default, "I would like to invite you to my LinkedIn Network." Instead, write something that engages the reader and reminds them of how you know each other. For example:

"I see from your profile that we both went on to become social workers. I'd like to get back in touch."

Or:

"Remember me? I'm the one that wrote those annoying two-page memos when we worked at B&G."

Vicki calls this type of message "rewarming the relationship."

EXCHANGE FAVORS

Both your connections (1st-degree) and people whom they could introduce you to (your 2nd-degree connections) become potential resources. If you have only 50 connections and your connections have an average of 100, you have 5,000 people whom you potentially could call on to help you with your job search. For example, you might ask:

"I see that you took the Certificate in Digital Marketing from PSU. Did you find the content up-to-date?"

Or:

"Would you mind spending a few minutes to talk to me about the work-life balance at Nike? I'm interested in applying for an IT job there."

You can extend job search help to your connections with offers such as:

"I just met the director of operations for Athletic Sporting Goods. He's a great guy! I know you're interested in working for that company. Shall I introduce you over LinkedIn?"

To build goodwill you might notice and send a message to your 1st-degree contacts acknowledging their accomplishments:

"Congratulations on your new position. I knew you had leadership chops!"

Remember, you've met and had positive interactions with hundreds of people who would like to help you network to find a new job. Why not make the most of this goodwill tool to allow your network to help you, maybe even in ways you never expected?

CONGRATULATIONS! YOU NOW HAVE A BASIC LINKEDIN PRESENCE. IT'S TIME FOR SOME GIFTS.

- *Go to an arts festival, a neighborhood street fair, or a farmers' market. If you're feeling social, make conversation with at least one person you've never met.*

- *Tell someone that you love them. In person is best, but over the phone is good, too.*

- *If you like to sing, set up a karaoke night with friends.*

LINKEDIN: EXPAND AND TAP YOUR NETWORK

Now that you've used LinkedIn to build a professional network of current friends and colleagues, we hope that you are starting to enjoy and understand the benefits of it. If so, you may want to go to the next level and strategically add new connections who share your desired job title or work in your target companies.

INVITE STRANGERS TO CONNECT

The purpose of inviting a stranger to connect is to build a relationship so you can potentially help each other with your careers. When you write your invitation, notice something about the person that interests you; maybe you have something or someone in common. Or, maybe you are interested in a company or organization where they currently (or even previously) work. An example of an invitation to a stranger might be:

"Hi Phil, I notice you worked for Mercy Corps. I love what they've done on their website with their action center. I'd like to connect."

Don't start out by making a request. Like all humans, people respond to others who take the time to listen and key into them. If Phil accepts your connection, the next step might be to ask him if you can buy him coffee and chat about Mercy Corps.

Once you've connected with someone in a **target organization**, you can ask questions like:

- What challenges are the organization facing that I could address in my cover letter or interview?

- What terminology is used within the organization? For example, when they refer to project management, should I use very specific terminology and metrics?

- Will I often have to work weekends at this company?

If you have built a solid relationship, you can ask if you could refer to them in your cover letter. Ideally, if they are well-positioned, they will pass your name on to the hiring manager or HR to keep an eye out for your resume.

Once you've connected with someone who has a **job title** to which you aspire, you can ask questions like:

- Which skills should I build that will make me more competitive?

- Who are the standout employers who hire people like us?

- Would you be willing to look at my LinkedIn profile to see if I could present my skills better?

FIND PEOPLE CONNECTED TO YOUR CONNECTIONS

When you are connected to someone (1st-degree), you can see their connections (2nd-degree). Go to **My Network** to display a list of your connections and then click on the person whose connections you want to view. On their profile page, click **See Connections** in the right-hand column, across from the **Message** button.

Connections are somewhat like cousins—you are probably close to your first cousins, know what they do professionally, and could tap them for a favor. You are also related to second cousins but less likely to know them and may want an introduction to build a relationship. This comparison holds true for connecting with 2nd-degree connections on LinkedIn—you can ask your 1st-degree connection to make an introduction, while putting in a good word for you.

If you've stayed in touch with your 1st-degree connection and believe they would want to be of

Joe wanted to explore working for "lighting" design firms, so Vicki suggested that he review her connections who had the keyword lighting in their profiles. He then reviewed their profiles and asked to connect, saying that Vicki suggested he reach out. As a result of ensuing informational interviews, he learned which lighting pieces to emphasize in his portfolio, which firms to target, and which professional conferences he might attend. Because he made a positive impression, these contacts put in a good word for him when openings became available with their employers.

assistance, you can make a request like this:

"Hi Gerry, I am excited about applying for the position as executive director of the Firk Family Foundation and want to do more research about the organization. I see you are connected to Dan Fischer, who was previously on the board. Would you be willing to introduce me to Dan?"

You can also reach out to 2nd-degree connections yourself, without an introduction, by sending a message that refers to your mutual contact and one other professional interest you have in common:

"Greetings Patty, I enjoyed reviewing your profile and see that you also have an interest in trauma-informed therapy. Since we have 11 contacts in common, it seems like we are in the same professional tribe, so I'd like to connect."

FIND PEOPLE BY TARGETED EMPLOYER

As part of your job search, we've encouraged you to identify approximately 15 companies that match your desired location, values, and industry. Most midsized and larger employers have a LinkedIn **company page**. Type the name of the company you want to research in the main search field and LinkedIn will show you a profile of the company as well as the profiles of people who work for them, once again indicating with a "2nd" if they are a 1st-degree connection to your contact.

Even if there are no people in this organization to whom you can be introduced, you can review employee profiles to see if you have a similar background to them. In addition, you can see which LinkedIn groups a person belongs to and then join those groups to build the relationship.

You can review your network on LinkedIn to see if anyone is working there by going to the upper-right corner of LinkedIn, changing the drop-down menu to **Companies**, and then searching for the company name. The screen that pops up will show anyone in your network who has listed the company as a current or past employer. You might want to contact them, following the Golden Rule for personalized invitations. If they respond, you can ask if they would like to chat on the phone and/or go out to tea.

FIND PEOPLE WITH DESIRED JOB TITLES

Another job search strategy is to reach out to new people who now hold the job titles that you are seeking, and the managers who hire people like you.

While still on the Connections page, enter a job title in the search field, such as "massage therapist" or "energy analyst." LinkedIn will show you the profiles of local individuals with these job titles. Look for the number 2 and begin by seeing if you have a mutual contact who can introduce you. Even if the person is a 3rd-degree connection, it may be useful to examine

THE GOLDEN RULE: CONNECT WITH A PERSONAL INVITATION

*When inviting people without an introduction, don't just hit the **Connect** button without sending a personalized invitation. Otherwise, the person will have no idea who you are or why you are interested in them and chances are good they will not accept your invitation. Make sure you review their profile and engage them around commonalities.*

their education and work experience and invite them to connect.

SLEUTH FOR WHAT YOU HAVE IN COMMON

Whether you locate new connections through your 1st-degree connections, through keywords in job titles, or through interests, you want to be thoughtful in crafting a short, personalized introduction. Reviewing their profile with genuine curiosity will help you find things you have in common (or affinities). You may find that you both:

- Worked to pass a land-use bill

- Are engineers from India

- Were in the Peace Corps in West Africa

- Share 20 of the same 1st-degree connections

- Worked for the same small company

- Went to the same prestigious college (all people with Ivy degrees help each other)

- Played the flute with an orchestra

- Are geeks who love the R programming language

- Follow Arianna Huffington as an influencer

- Went to the same small undergraduate or graduate program

Nearly everyone responds to an invitation that highlights what you have in common, so taking the extra time to get to know someone through their profile is worth it.

ADDRESS YOUR RESERVATIONS

We know that reaching out to people you've never met can be awkward and may seem intrusive, especially for introverts. It helps to remember that LinkedIn is designed for this very purpose—to build relationships with people who share common educational and professional interests and goals. Therefore, from a "LinkedIn point of view," asking a stranger to connect is not unseemly at all—just remember to use the Golden Rule of LinkedIn invitations and you'll be fine.

"Successful people are always looking for opportunities to help others. Unsuccessful people are always asking, 'What's in it for me?'"
—Brian Tracy

Step 5
Interview with Confidence

"One important key to success is self-confidence. An important key to self-confidence is preparation." —Arthur Ashe

INTRODUCTION

You've selected and applied for a compelling job at a great organization. Your top-notch resume and cover letter achieved the goal of landing you an interview. Congratulations—your hard work has paid off!

Now you are faced with the interview process, which for some—especially the introverts among us—can be a terrifying prospect. One of Leslie's clients even said, "I'd rather have a root canal than face an interview panel." We can relate! Going into your interviews fully prepared helps calm the interview jitters, allowing you to channel your anxiety into excitement for meeting new people and learning about a new company.

The first step to successful interviewing is doing your research and being clear about your strengths. In **Prepare for the Interview** we offer research tips and help you decide which strengths you want to highlight in your interview.

In this day and age, the interview process commonly begins with a phone screen and might include a conversation over Skype, GoToMeeting, or some other virtual meeting tool. In **Phone and Video Interviews**, we offer tips and tricks for making it through these types of interviews.

Common Interview Questions lists the behavioral questions that are currently in vogue and offers suggestions for questions you might ask the employer. In **Tell a Story in CAR (Challenge, Action, Results) Format** we provide guidelines for framing your answers in a "Challenge, Action, and Results" format that leaves an impression. In **Answer the Question: What Are Your Weaknesses?** you learn how to handle this difficult question with poise and confidence.

Presenting your strengths in an assured yet polite manner as well as showing interest in your future manager goes a long way toward landing you a job offer. We included Vicki's blog article titled **Brag Politely, but Make Your Potential Boss #1** to show you how to brag effectively while making the interviewer the star of the show.

You may want to pay special attention to **Interviewing for the Older Candidate** if you are concerned about ageism. In **Interviewing for the Overqualified Candidate** we stress how to showcase your skills in a way that offsets the manager's concerns that you will be bored or leave soon.

What Should I Wear? helps you plan your outfit and offers grooming tips to present your most attractive self to the interview. Finally, **Interview Thank-You** describes how to write a thank-you note that keeps you fresh in the hiring manager's mind so that you are invited back or, if you've had the final interview, receive a job offer.

After you set aside time to prepare and practice, we encourage you to engage in your favorite self-care activities prior to the interview. A relaxing massage, yoga with meditation, or a vigorous run can help you calm your nerves, ensuring you show up poised and confident!

PREPARE FOR THE INTERVIEW

An interview is an important performance and there are no second chances. Even if you decide later that you don't want the job, at this point you have only one goal: to win an offer. Being nervous is natural. The real issue is how to convert your nervous energy into productive action. Fortunately, there is a lot you can do to improve your performance. Preparation falls into three areas: research, strategy, and practice.

DO YOUR RESEARCH

When you are offered an in-person interview ask how many people will be interviewed, the names and positions of the interviewers, and how long the interview is expected to take. This will give you an idea if this is a screening interview (i.e., six candidates for 30 minutes) or a final interview (i.e., three candidates with the hiring manager for an hour).

The ease of the internet makes initial research simple and an absolute must. If you haven't studied the company website before the interview, you send the message that you don't care much about the job. A company website tells you what the employer wants people to think and feel about the organization. For example, "We are the technological leader in our field." For another perspective, research the organization online. *The Portland Business Journal,* for example, may show you what others have said about the organization. **Glassdoor.com** is not only a job board but an excellent source for testimonials and reviews from people who have actually worked at the company or interviewed for jobs there.

If you know the names of the individuals who will be interviewing you, go ahead and Google them, as well as search for their LinkedIn profiles. You might find professional articles they have written, presentations they have given, or if they belong to any LinkedIn groups. In addition to learning about them professionally, you might discover a mutual interest about which you could initiate small talk to create common ground quickly. For example, if you learn that your prospective manager is a judge for cat shows and you love cats, you can mention your tabby.

Researching prospective employers is yet another place where having a strong network is an asset. You can ask your connections if anyone knows anyone at the organization. This can give you access to information such as pet peeves or personal style of the supervisor. For example, one of Vicki's clients used her network to learn that the IT manager who would supervise her was very bottom-line oriented. Therefore, she was able to practice CAR (challenge, action, results) statements that gave examples of her bottom-line outcomes in clear quantitative terms. See *Tell a Story in CAR (Challenge, Action, Results) Format* for more information.

DEVISE A STRATEGY

After you understand as much as you can about the perceived needs of the employer, decide which of your strengths should be accentuated in the interview. Vicki calls her approach "Three by Two." First, choose three strengths that you want to convey during the interview. These strengths should align closely with what you believe is important to the employer for this position. Then, develop two examples (CAR statements) for each strength.

These strengths will determine the basic themes you want to convey throughout the interview. This message ideally matches the Professional Profile section on your resume. For example, if your Professional Profile says, "Imaginative and artistic user experience expert with over 15 years in developing designs that are friendly and intuitive. Out-of-the-box thinker who enjoys collaborating with others to innovate the best user experience possible," you will stick to this theme about your professional

---

Tip

*It is never too late to research salary ranges. If you get invited back for another interview, we recommend you begin this research now (see **Salary Research**) so you are well prepared if you get an offer.*

DO NOT TALK ABOUT SALARY AT AN INTERVIEW

Wait until after you've received an offer before discussing salary. If the interviewer asks what your salary requirements are, simply say, "I trust that if you choose to offer me the position, you will offer a salary that is fair market value for my job duties." You don't want to quote a figure that is too low and then get stuck being paid less than is fair. Conversely, you don't want to price yourself out of getting an offer. We discuss strategies for negotiating compensation later in this handbook.

approach throughout the interview. When the employer sees and hears the same message, it sticks.

Plan an approach on how to handle your weaknesses and any questions that you fear. The general rule is to answer questions about them but to minimize the amount of time you spend on those answers. In other words, act like a politician who responds quickly to questions and then moves back on topic. In your case, your three strengths are "on topic." Because the "weakness" question can create the most amount of anxiety during the interview, we go into more detail about this question in *Answer the Question: What Are Your Weaknesses?*

We always encourage people to present themselves as nothing but enthusiastic about a position and initially to bite their tongues about reservations. Reservations can be brought up after you are offered a position. You have much more power once the employer has decided that you are the best person to meet their needs. They will be more motivated to consider possible changes to address your reservations after they see you as part of the solution to their problems.

Once you have an offer in hand, you can ask for a meeting to address your concerns head-on. Fortunately, job offers are not customarily rescinded during the negotiation process, even if there are some points of contention. To put it simply, in the formal interview they decide if they want you; in this second meeting, you finally decide if you want them.

PRACTICE

Practice! Practice! Practice! This is the key to the successful interview. Identify the most important skills and character traits you have to offer that match each of the employer's needs. Identify the points that you want to get across in the interview no matter the specific questions asked. Review your CAR statements on your resume and be prepared to elaborate on these.

Practicing in front of people will convert a strong strategy into a strong performance, which will make a powerful impression of your strengths on the interviewer. Every job seeker who has rehearsed with Vicki or her associates, either in an individual session or in a small-group interview clinic, has noticeably grown in competence and confidence. One participant who competed well for a marketing communications position at TriMet said, "Because I was well prepared, I could relax. This allowed me to use humor to warm the relationship with the interviewers." She won the offer!

PHONE AND VIDEO INTERVIEWS

Don't be surprised if your first interview is on the phone or online—for example, over Skype or Google Hangouts. A phone or online interview is a common method human resources employees use to screen candidates for hiring managers. The way you prepare for these interviews is generally the same as for in-person interviews, but with a few caveats.

PHONE INTERVIEWS

Phone interviews allow you to have a conversation with a company representative while enjoying your morning coffee in your pajamas or before showering after your morning workout. Nevertheless, there are a few things to keep in mind to ensure a successful phone interview.

A quiet location and convenient time: When you get a call from a company to which you've sent a resume, find a quiet place to talk. If you do not know it is the company calling and you have answered the phone in a noisy place, you can excuse yourself while you move to a quiet location. If you are in the middle of something else or heading out the door, it's perfectly acceptable to say, "Thank you so much for calling. I'm heading out the door to an appointment, would it be convenient for you if I call you tomorrow at 10 a.m.?" It is important for you to devote 100 percent of your attention to the company representative on the phone.

Body stance: Speak directly into the phone with the mouthpiece about one inch away. Smile while speaking. This adds an enthusiastic and energetic tone to your voice. Take the call standing up or pace if you need to. This helps with breathing, dispels nerves, and elevates your confidence. If you are a kinesthetic type, pacing will help you organize your thoughts and think creatively.

Hold up your end of the conversation: Respond with interest to the company representative's statements. Simple phrases like, "oh, that's interesting," "yes, I see," "uh-huh," "okay," and "great" are verbal equivalents to the positive body language you will show when you get the in-person interview.

Ask questions: Let the representative guide the interview, but if there is a break or they ask you if you have any questions, be prepared! Remember that recruiters do not know the answers to technical questions. Here are some questions that will help you learn more about the job:

- What made me stand out as a candidate for this job?

- From your perspective, what is the company culture like?

- Which projects will I be the most involved with during the first six months?

- What type of person succeeds in this job and why?

- What are the biggest challenges the department faces this year and what will my role be in addressing them?

VIDEO INTERVIEWS

Because video interviews over applications like Skype, Zoom, or Google Hangouts are becoming more and more popular, we highly recommend you set up a Skype, Zoom, or Google Hangouts account if you have not done so already. If you are not used to video calls, set up some with friends or relatives until you are comfortable with the technology.

Dress the part and prepare the stage: Make sure that your hair and face are groomed, and you are professionally dressed, at least from the waist up. Because the company representative will be looking at you against a background, make sure it is clean and tidy; a plain blank wall behind you is usually the best way to go.

Kim, a client of Leslie's, was asked to video record herself answering a series of questions and then send the recording to the HR employee. The same principles apply to these "one-sided" video interviews." Just pretend the interviewer is on the other end of your screen; answer the questions as if you were talking to a real person, remembering to smile and be engaging.

Look into the camera lens: A common mistake during a video session is to stare at the interviewer's onscreen image. From the interviewer's perspective, you are looking down which can give the impression you are avoiding eye contact—not the message you want to convey. The lens is usually at the top center of your laptop screen. Position your laptop so that the lens is at your eye level and then train yourself to look directly into it.

Even with the best intentions, you will find yourself looking at the screen from time to time. Just remember to make an extra effort to look at the camera lens when:

- You say hello

- The interviewer is asking you a question

- You ask a question

- You are making an important point

- You are concluding an answer

- The interview is wrapping up and you are saying your good-byes

Put a smile on your face: Just as you would during an in-person interview, smile and appear engaged in the conversation.

END WELL AND LEAVE AN IMPRESSION

The phone or video interview usually ends with the company representative asking you if you have any questions. They may even ask you directly, "What would you like to know about us?" This is the perfect time to ask the questions listed above.

Video interviews are not only conducted by a company representative in HR but are sometimes conducted by hiring managers who want to screen candidates for in-person interviews. If you are interviewing with a hiring manager, now is the time to get specific and technical with your questions:

- What kind of challenges are you currently facing meeting sales quotas?

- I understand you are moving your web services to the cloud. What challenges are you anticipating during this transition?

- I read that you were looking to update your office technology. Can you tell me in which direction you plan on going?

- I'm excited to apply my knowledge of the latest features of Java. How specifically can I help?

Having this type of information helps you package your skills to fully match the needs of the company before the in-person interview. You can wrap up the conversation with, "This sounds like a very interesting and exciting opportunity, Ms. Smith, and one in which I believe I could definitely contribute. What are the next steps?"

Tip

Maintaining eye contact online takes practice. We recommend enlisting the help of a friend or family member.

When an invitation for an in-person interview is extended you'll want to know:

- How many interviews typically occur before a decision is made?

- Who will be part of the interview team and what are their roles within the department?

- What is your time frame for filling the position?

- Can you give me an idea of which critical areas will be discussed?

The last piece of information you want to gather is the correct spelling and pronunciation of the interviewer's name and their email address so that you can send a follow-up thank-you note or email. Don't wait longer than 24 hours to send this note. Include what struck you most about the company during your conversation and that you look forward to meeting _____ at the in-person interview.

After the phone or video screening interview, you may get a sense that the job isn't the right one for you. Nevertheless, you might still want to go through the next step of the interview process; it is excellent practice and you never know the full extent of a position from the initial phone call. It may turn out to be the perfect job!

THE GIFT OF CONVERSATION

Open up to a partner or close friend about your deepest insecurities related to your job search or interviewing. It will help you process your thoughts before you face your first interviewer.

Behavioral questions are in vogue, which means that questions often begin with "Tell me about a time..." or "Describe a time when..." Practice answering the following common questions:

- Why are you interested in this position?

- Why are you interested in this company?

- Tell me about yourself.

- Where do you expect to be in three years?

- Describe a time that you were part of a team and your role as a team member.

- Describe a conflict you had on a job and how you resolved it.

- What have been your most important accomplishments?

- What are your strengths? Give an example of your strengths in action.

- What are your weaknesses?

- Give us an example of a time when you faced a difficult challenge.

- Why should we hire you?

QUESTIONS YOU ASK THE EMPLOYER

At the end of most interviews you will be asked, "Do you have any questions you would like to ask us?" You should prepare a list of six to ten questions in advance. You usually won't ask more than three or four, but because several of your questions may be covered during the interview, you don't want to run out.

There are three interrelated goals you want to meet when you ask your questions:

1. You genuinely want to learn more about the organization and the position to decide if you want to accept an offer, if one is extended.

2. You want to ask intelligent questions that show you have done your research into the position and/or organization.

3. You want to demonstrate your outstanding listening skills.

It is human nature for people to bond with those who listen and express interest in their ideas and concerns. This ability to listen can be demonstrated verbally and nonverbally through body posture and facial expressions. The technique of **reflective** or **active listening** can be quite effective in building rapport. The listener reflects on key elements of the feeling and content of the interviewer's message.

Examples that might be appropriate in an interview situation include:

- You sound concerned about the stresses caused by an outdated computer system. I'm interested in hearing more about this.

- Am I hearing you correctly that one of your biggest concerns is the lack of qualified individuals available to implement the new programs your department needs?

The following questions demonstrate your desire to understand the concerns and perspectives of the people who are selecting a new employee:

- How do you see the organization changing over the next few years? I've had a chance to review the strategic plan on your website. Do you see it as realistic and on track?

- Wh t are the goals of this department and how would the person you choose to fill this position contribute?

- What would the top priority be for me to accomplish in the first six months if I am selected for this position?

- I read that you have been very successful at _____. What do you think accounts for this success?

- I know that Concordia is a leader in providing access for adults returning to school, including the use of computer-based distance learning. What accounts for your leadership in this arena?

- I read that 3JConsulting is one of the fastest growing civil engineering companies in Portland. To what do you attribute your growth?

 GIVE YOURSELF THE GIFT OF EXERCISE AND RELAXATION

Go for a swim at the local community center and then relax in the hot tub or sauna after.

TELL A STORY IN CAR (CHALLENGE, ACTION, RESULTS) FORMAT

The purpose of telling a story during the interview is to illustrate your skills and accomplishments with a vivid example. An effective story begins by identifying the **challenge** (C) you faced in your professional activities. It then tells of the **action** (A) you took to resolve the problem. It concludes with the **results** (R) you achieved for the organization.

FIRST, REVIEW YOUR ACCOMPLISHMENTS

To identify possible accomplishments to use as a basis for a CAR story, consider these questions. Are you proud that you:

- Developed something? (A product? A procedure? A news release? A video?)

- Reduced costs or improved efficiency?

- Improved morale and teamwork?

- Surpassed an accepted standard for quality or quantity of performance?

- Gained new customers? Retained old customers?

- Improved operations to increase productivity or reduce stress?

- Received informal recognition or formal awards?

CHALLENGE (C)

State the problem *before* you talk about the action(s) you took to improve it. Your research of the potential employer will help you identify the types of challenges this company faces that are like those you have addressed in the past. You might explain the problem in ways like the descriptions below:

- There was a lot of interdepartmental conflict and disorganization in the areas of _____.

- Most of the youth served by the NE Council for Drug and Alcohol were African-American, while only one of the 15 counselors was African-American.

- The number of donors was ___ percent lower than anticipated.

- Expenses were too high, running ___ percent over budget.

- People in the community were not aware of the availability of curbside recycling.

- Clients regularly complained about _____.

- Deadlines were missed on _____.

ACTIONS (A)

Describe what you did individually and/or your role in actions taken by a team. Begin with action verbs such as *improved, initiated, resolved, created, facilitated, sold,* or *wrote.* Give enough details of what you said and did so the interviewer can "see" you in action. You might comment on why you took this action.

Note: Actions often demonstrate the skills identified on your resume.

You might describe your actions in the following ways:

- I interviewed members to create a survey to measure customer satisfaction.

- I initiated a call campaign of past members.

Tip

Does the CAR approach sound familiar to you? It should—it is essentially what you do in an abbreviated form when you describe your achievements on your resume. Refer to your resume to guide your CAR stories so that you deliver a consistent message as to why you are the perfect person for the job.

- I created a spreadsheet to compare costs and services of different promotional activities.

- I led a retreat where we revisited and recommitted to our vision and mission.

- I advertised in the *Skanner* and used my connections in NE Portland churches to recruit new African-American counselors.

- I spearheaded a campaign that included multimedia, multilingual outreach using direct mail, speeches, and advertising.

RESULTS (R)

Results are the positive outcomes of your actions. They provide the *after* picture in contrast to the *before* picture presented as the challenge. Private companies and many nonprofits are driven by the bottom line, so results are impressive if you directly increased profits or decreased costs. You might have had an indirect impact on profits or costs by increasing efficiency, attracting more customers, reducing customer attrition, or introducing new services or programs.

Some positions lend themselves to measurable results or an estimate of measurable results. Your results could include one or several positive outcomes like the examples below:

- By calling inactive members, I increased membership by 22 percent.

- By running an effective campaign, I helped elect Green Party Candidate Sharon Ball.

- By training new employees more effectively, the number of complaints was reduced by 20 percent.

- The retreat increased morale so that only one staff member left during the year, compared to four during the previous year.

- I increased diversity and served more clients of color by adding three new African-American counselors to the staff.

Nonprofits, government, and educational institutions are often impressed with results related to the organization's mission, standards, or performance. Examples:

- Because I helped introduce a new program, the reading scores of students in my third-grade class surpassed those of other third-grade students in the district.

- Because my weekly meetings improved morale so significantly, my supervisor rated me as "exceeds expectations" on all aspects of my communication skills, including my ability to resolve conflict.

- Because of my outreach efforts, we doubled the Hispanic community's involvement in parks and recreation programs.

PUT THE PARTS TOGETHER

You can draft your CARs by putting the three parts together and then adding the details, as shown in these examples:

- Most of the youth served by the NE Council for Drug and Alcohol were African-American, while only one of the 15 counselors was African-American (C). I advertised in the *Skanner* and used my connections in NE Portland churches (A) to recruit three new African-American counselors (R).

- The Montana Arts Council had poor communication with its donors, its customers, and the public (C). I created an electronic newsletter and permission-based email system (A). As a result, the number of donors increased by 22 percent (R).

- The City of San Jose hired my company, Peynet Public Relations, to persuade residents to participate in an expanded curbside recycling program (C). I created a comprehensive multimedia,

multilingual outreach campaign using direct mail, publicity, a speaker's bureau, school assemblies, and advertising (A). The recycling volume tripled, exceeding the goal of doubling (R).

- There was a high turnover rate in our department. Employees were complaining that "the right hand didn't know what the left hand was doing" and left the company in frustration. This resulted in missed deadlines and higher costs (C). I initiated weekly, cross-departmental meetings with key players on the project and started an email group to improve communication (A). The feedback from the employees was positive and increased retention such that deadlines were met. My manager rated me as "exceeds expectations" on my ability to meet project requirements and on communications skills (R).

Tip

*You can use the **Draft Your Accomplishments** worksheet in **Step 3: Prepare Your Resume and Cover Letter** to prepare CAR statements for your interview. Instead of leading with the result like you did on your resume, you'll lead with the challenge when telling your CAR story.*

ANSWER THE QUESTION: WHAT ARE YOUR WEAKNESSES?

We've all been there. We're breezing through the job interview, and then we get the dreaded question: "Tell us about your weaknesses." Hmmm...A tricky question to be sure. You want to choose an authentic answer, but you don't want to hurt your candidacy. Take a tip from politicians—briefly respond to the sticky question, then pivot back to your major strengths.

There are several approaches you can take to handle the dreaded "weakness" question:

- **Address the obvious.** For example, you might lead with, "You noted in the job description that you would prefer a candidate who speaks Spanish, and I do not speak Spanish." Then, you could continue with an example of your sensitivity to Hispanic culture or involvement in that community.

- **Reframe as a positive.** One of our clients was meticulous about deadlines and frequently checked on her team's progress. In her interview she admitted, "Some have taken this to mean that I do not trust them. I have learned to minimize this reaction by telling everyone at the start that these check-ins are part of standard procedure. Then they do not take it personally."

- **Draw on context.** A perceived weakness in one position might be a strength in another. Acknowledge the perceived weakness, then explain why you think it would be a strength in the new work culture or environment. For example, "In the past, employers haven't wanted me to consult with my team before making decisions. I have chosen to apply to your company because of your reputation for inclusive decision-making."

- **Highlight improvement.** Tell how you identified the weakness and then acted to turn it into a strength. "I used to avoid public speaking like the flu. That changed last year when I started Toastmasters. Now, I am proud to say that I speak at public meetings several times a month and that my presentations get rave reviews."

KNOW YOUR ANSWER AND HOW YOU'LL SAY IT

Practice with a career professional or in front of friends. Ask for feedback on your body posture and tone of voice when you address your weakness. Sit tall and don't sound apologetic. Ask them if you have convincingly turned the weakness question into an opportunity to present your resilience and strengths. Keep practicing until you've convinced your audience that you are a strong, confident candidate who is self-aware and knows how to grow personally and professionally.

The interview is the time and place where you get to put your best self forward. That includes not only highlighting your skills and achievements but also making the person who sits across from you feel good about themselves. Are you a team player who is willing to support her boss by taking on some extra tasks during crunch time? Do you like to collaborate and innovate together with your colleagues and your manager? Remember those professional themes on your resume and carry those messages into the interview to make you shine!

BRAG POLITELY

Most people find it uncomfortable to talk about their achievements, fearful that they might be perceived as a braggart. It is imperative to change this mindset, especially when engaged in a job search. How else are you going to convey your knowledge, skills, and abilities to a potential employer? Instead of thinking about sharing accomplishments as bragging, keep the focus on your goal—sharing what you have to offer to solve the employer's problems.

The reality is you need to brag about yourself in an interview. You can do so without being a jerk by emphasizing your distinct qualities and experience while addressing the employer's challenges. "Easier said than done," you say? Consider these three suggestions for tooting your own horn.

1. **Cite a third party.** "I consistently get top marks for _____ in my performance reviews," or "while working at Acme Inc., I regularly heard positive feedback about my ____." You're not bragging, you're simply repeating what others have said about you. Social proof like this helps your interviewer believe, "If she got that praise from her last employer, then she'll be an excellent addition to our team."

2. **State your strengths as passions.** There's a reason you're interested in this position. What is it? "I'm passionate about (talents related to the job's responsibilities)." Describe how your professional interests align with the job and you'll imply that your performance is driven by more than a paycheck.

3. **Practice your answers.** By the time you get to the interview stage, you should have a good idea of the questions that you'll be asked (see *Common Interview Questions* for a review). Remember the professional themes and accomplishment statements on your resume? Plan to weave those into your answers. Ask a friend or family member to help you practice. If this isn't possible, practice in front of a mirror so you can make sure you sound and look confident!

MAKE YOUR FUTURE BOSS THE MOST IMPORTANT PERSON IN THE INTERVIEW

It's a rare day when Vicki gets a finger wag from one of her clients. The wobbly digit came from Cris, a straight-talking New Yorker seeking a nonprofit job in Portland. In interviews, Cris had been asked how she would handle a difference of opinion with her boss. Cris's rapid-fire practice answer included a finger wag and the statement: "I'd go behind closed doors, give my honest opinion, and expect him or her to respect mine. Then, if he or she won, I'd go out and show public support."

This answer had some strength to it, but it reflected two mistakes in Cris's delivery:

- Even in her practice answer, Cris shook her finger in a scolding gesture. Most bosses want sharp, intelligent associates who feel welcome to be honest but without the wagging finger. It hints at a possible role reversal.

- Cris's win/lose metaphor played to the stereotype that New Yorkers are aggressive—not an ideal impression to make in Portland's laid-back nonprofit community.

In job interviews, it's natural for the candidate to think of him or herself as the center of the meeting—and that's how most job candidates behave. So, imagine the impression you'd make on your prospective boss if you redirected the spotlight. Here are four tips to help you do that:

1. Pause a little longer. Take a hint from Midwestern mannerisms. Research has shown that Midwesterners leave a longer pause after someone stops speaking—nearly twice as long as a New Yorker's speedy reply. Pausing after the interviewer speaks shows that you are interested in his or her thoughts, you're really letting them sink in, and you're waiting to see if they'll tell you more. Who wouldn't feel flattered?

2. Do your research. It's human nature for people to bond with those who show interest in their ideas and concerns. Research your interviewer on LinkedIn, including articles they have posted in groups. Then, reveal this effort with relevant questions about their priorities and professional approach. It's fine to refer directly to what you learned from LinkedIn—this is considered research rather than snooping.

3. Exude interest. In addition to asking relevant questions and expressing verbal enthusiasm, show your engagement and interest through your eyes and your smile. During the interview make eye contact with everyone in the room, giving special attention to your future boss.

4. Send the right nonverbal signals. Only a sliver of any message is in the words. Practice greater awareness of the nonverbal messages that you're conveying, intentionally or otherwise. Maintain an open body posture—no folded arms, crossed legs, or furrowed brows. Again, solicit the help of a friend or family member, or practice in front of the mirror and take note of what your body is saying.

Instead of viewing these suggestions as an invitation to be fake, think of them as ways to show genuine interest in the boss. Also, remember your pride in what you bring to the table—and leave the wagging fingers at home.

INTERVIEWING FOR THE OLDER CANDIDATE

If you are over 50, chances are you possess a wealth of experience, knowledge, and wisdom that can provide great benefit to any company or organization. Nevertheless, ageism is alive and well in American culture and the trick is to get past those younger interviewers' unconscious biases.

If your research indicates that you will be supervised by a much younger person, carry out a "cross-cultural" study prior to the interview. What does their generation wear? What vocabulary do they use? What do they read? What social media platforms do they like? What applications do they use? Or better yet, what shows do they watch? With this preparation, you won't be as likely to use a word that makes you seem old-fashioned. If you forget a detail about a past project or task you performed, don't cover up with a reference to having a "senior moment."

A second way to counteract covert age prejudice is to tell stories with cleverly embedded messages that working for someone younger is no problem:

Interviewer: "Can you give me an example of a challenge you faced?"

You: "I was leading a team of writers and graphic designers to create a newsletter intended to raise funds for the library. I sent the plans to my manager and she had signed off. On Friday, however, when the team was well underway, she returned from a national conference with the news that the best donors are now in the 35-to-45-year-old set rather than their grandparents. I worked over the weekend and on Monday morning presented my manager with three new edgy looks, one of which I adapted from the *Sex in the City* logo. She was delighted she didn't have to work late and was able to pick up her child from Montessori right on time."

In two minutes, you have landed darts into two puffed-up legends: the IPBOP (Iron-Poor Blood Old Person) legend and the ODNTA (Old Dog, New Trick Aversion) legend. You have also demonstrated that you are respectful to your younger "superiors."

You will seem more out-of-date if you are not up on the technology they use. For example, if you're a whiz on Lotus 1-2-3 or Quark, don't mention it. One older interviewee was asked about her background with technology. When she began by saying, "When I started, back when there were punch cards..." she was inadvertently labeling herself as a dinosaur. Get current, and let your future employer know that you are competent in the required technical skills.

A last bit of interview advice is to present yourself as a responsive listener, eager to learn from your manager and colleagues. You can achieve this by communicating as if you come from the Midwest. It has been proven that Midwesterners leave a longer polite pause after someone stops speaking, nearly twice as long as the New Yorker's speeding-bullet response. The Midwestern approach gives the speaker the impression that you are terribly interested in their pearls of wisdom and are pausing to see if they wish to tell you more.

BUILD GOODWILL AND ADDRESS THE ELEPHANT IN THE ROOM

When the interviewer asks you a closing question like, "Do you have any questions for us, Gertrude?" this is an invitation to build mutual feelings of ease across the generational divide. You can say, "Justin, I was impressed with your analysis of the budget. Can you tell me more about your thinking, so I can know how I can help you reach your goal?"

This is also the perfect time to address the age issue head-on. You could say:

"Justin, if I were you interviewing me, a seasoned

Tip

When answering questions in which you refer to a previous manager, make them the same gender as your future manager or, if that's not possible, make them gender neutral.

professional, I might have several age-related questions I think I shouldn't ask. I might be wondering about energy, drive, manageability, and how well you'd get along with a team that looks to be 20 years younger. And I'd be thinking about your ability to keep up with current trends. If you're wondering any of these things, I'd love to address this now, if I may."

You can then discuss the advantages of your age:

- You have lived through crises, emergencies, and unexpected outcomes on the job. You know how to handle it all without batting an eye and have learned from the lessons in each situation.

- You are not looking to change jobs in four years like many younger candidates are. You simply want to find an excellent team, settle into the position, and come to be known as a trusted employee that your manager and team can count on.

- You won't be looking for quick promotions or instant raises; instead, you'll be viewed as a loyal employee who possesses the three C's: calmness, competence, and conscientiousness.

- At the request of your manager, you will make yourself available to mentor younger team members and stabilize the team.

You do not necessarily have to wait until the end of the interview to raise these points. If you suspect at any time that the interviewer is concerned about your age, go ahead and address this when the opportunity arises. However, don't spend too much time focused on age. When the timing feels right, move off the age issue by asking a question that goes to the heart of the job and its deliverables.

If you feel as if you are putting yourself through too many contortions simply to please, you might think, "What the heck! They either want the real me or they don't." This can be a risky approach unless you have a sure source of income. Ultimately, keep in mind that by using these techniques you have presented your wise professional self in the best way possible—and, don't forget that they'd be lucky to have you!

VICKI'S EXPERIENCE

Vicki confesses that she was once a young manager with a wobbly ego. The finalists for the assistant director position were Clare—a very tall, poised, and exacting professional from Chicago—or Heidi, a petite, quiet woman from Burns, Oregon. Vicki had several of the worries we describe here about Clare, so she decided on Heidi, even though Heidi's expertise was not as deep, and she had misspelled liaison in her cover letter. Vicki later regretted the cost of her insecurity because she had to work harder and do more damage control than if she had just had the confidence to hire someone with more expertise than her.

The challenges of the older candidate and the overqualified candidate are very similar because both might present somewhat of a threat to a manager. A hiring manager might harbor the unexpressed prejudice that the candidate will:

- Get bored and leave soon.

- Still be looking for a better-paying position and leave soon.

- Criticize the way things are done based on their greater expertise.

- Be resistant to supervision.

- Steal some of the accolades that the hiring manager covets.

- Expect more raises and perks.

Management could conclude it is better for the company in the long run to hire someone of more modest capabilities.

OFFSET THE EMPLOYER'S CONCERNS
Fears about longevity, boredom, and a possible reversal of roles between the supervisor and employee are at the heart of discrimination for older and overqualified candidates alike. If you are overqualified, you can use some of the same tactics as the older candidate. For more information, see *Interviewing for the Older Candidate* for recommendations and examples of how to present yourself as smart, responsive to supervision, and nonthreatening.

It is particularly important to offset the fear that you will be a short-timer. There is no law that prevents the interviewer from directly asking you about the job's ability to satisfy your long-term career wishes. A question such as, "Why would you want this position, given that the compensation and challenges are lower than your previous positions?" is perfectly acceptable. There are several answers to avoid, although they may be true. "I need a root canal and this company has great dental benefits," or "It is a great stepping stone. I figure that once I am inside as a proofreader you will see my brilliance, and I will become the marketing director next year," are not responses that will land you an offer.

Better responses include:

- I've been reflecting for the last year on what is most important to me in my career. I've decided my top two criteria are working with a team and helping the environment. Although my old position had some positive aspects, this one meets my criteria in a much better way.

- I am concerned about the direction of the country. I want to commit myself to an organization and position that shares my passion for social justice.

- After ten years managing a design team, I discovered that I truly missed the creativity and artistic side of doing designs myself. I want to return to doing what I love, which is working collaboratively with others to come up with and implement stellar designs.

DO YOUR RESEARCH TO IMPRESS THE MANAGER

Search for articles your prospective manager has written or posted on social media and mention them during the interview. This will demonstrate an interest in their professional contributions to the field and indicate you will respect their professional guidance. If you dig deeper, you can find out how long your prospective manager has been with the company and discover their accomplishments during their tenure. This acknowledgment will demonstrate your interest in their priorities and direction, ideally resulting in an offer!

GIFTS TO SPICE UP YOUR LOOK FOR THE INTERVIEW

- *Treat yourself to a snappy new pair of shoes or item of clothing for your interview.*

- *Visit the salon or barber and get a trim or touch up those roots.*

HOW CLOTHES CAN MISSPEAK

We had a client who came from an upper-class old Portland family. She dressed attractively in clothing from shops like Nordstrom, wore tasteful gold jewelry, and had well-manicured red fingernails. She went to an interview for a fund-raising position for which she was highly qualified. She assumed her dress style would be a fit with the donors she would be approaching as part of her job. When she arrived at the interview, the three interviewers had silver ethnic jewelry and looked as if their clothes were a mix from REI and Goodwill. She believed the cool reception she received, including the subsequent rejection, conveyed, "We do not see you as fitting in with our culture."

Author Alison Lurie says, "Clothes never stop talking." There is a clear message that you want your clothes to convey in an interview. Whether you wear jeans or a tailored suit, the message needs to be: "I fit in. I am from your clan." When Vicki worked for a creative staffing agency where they placed people in edgy ad agencies, a man came in for an interview wearing a navy three-piece suit. They sent him to a bank instead.

It is helpful to take the perspective of the people hiring you. It does not mean that they are superficial if how you're dressed matters to them. They are trying to figure out from this brief encounter if you will be a good fit for their team. People are hardwired to feel more comfortable with people who look and act like them. They intuit—whether right or wrong—that values and work style will be compatible.

The general rule of thumb is to dress slightly more professionally than the person/people interviewing you. To dress one level up, you first need to find out what people generally wear in the work setting; you can visit their website or do some research on social media. One client noted that employees on the company's website and on their LinkedIn profiles wore shirts without ties. He used this clue to dress accordingly.

For men, there is a pyramid of interview attire, from jeans to suits.

- If your future manager is likely to be wearing jeans, it is safe for you to wear Dockers and a dress shirt without a tie.

- If he will be wearing Dockers and a dress shirt without a tie, you can wear Dockers with a collared shirt and a jacket.

- If he will be wearing dress slacks with a button-up shirt and a jacket without a tie, you can wear the same with a tie.

- If he is wearing a button-up shirt, slacks, a jacket, and a tie, and it is a conventional business environment, you can wear a suit with a button-up shirt and a conservative tie. If the one suit that you have is old, browse through Men's Wearhouse to see if your lapels, pant length, etc., are totally out of style or retro chic (back in fashion once again).

Women have more choices of clothing combinations, including some that men have (slacks and blouse or traditional pantsuits), as well as skirts and dresses. This makes it harder to create a parallel interview attire pyramid for women, but the same principles apply. In Portland, generally you are safe with a nice skirt, blouse, and jacket.

Jewelry is perfectly fine if it is subtle and tasteful. Avoid pieces that are oversized, too sparkly or dangly, or have religious symbols or your name or initials on them. Makeup is also fine as long as it follows

WHAT IF YOUR STYLE DOES NOT CONFORM TO GENDER NORMS?

Most sectors of Portland are LGBTQ friendly and do not discriminate against women whose style is more masculine. However, some transgender candidates and men whose styles lean towards the traditionally feminine may experience discrimination. In these cases, you will need to choose how you present yourself: do you dress according to expectation, or do you dress to express your unique and true self, knowing that if the company likes who you are, that is what matters?

the same rules as jewelry: it is subtle and tastefully applied.

Peruse the photographs on LinkedIn, particularly the managers', to find out the company's level of formality or casualness. Sometimes it's even fun to drop by the organization to get a feel for the people and their culture. In creative environments, people often have fun with their clothing and may even sport a tattoo or two. If, however, you are interviewing for a corporate job in a formal environment, you may choose to hide any tattoos or piercings outside of the traditional single-pierced ears for women. And if you do have those single-pierced ears, you can wear small, tasteful earrings for conventional environments.

Bottom Line: you do not want assumptions about your appearance to detract from the central issue—your ability to do the job.

PERSONAL GROOMING AND HYGIENE

Personal grooming of hair, skin, teeth, and nails is straightforward, but body odor might take some extra thought. Foods like onions, garlic, cilantro, and fried and greasy items can give off an unpleasant pungent smell. It's a good idea to consider your diet at the same time you are assembling your interview wardrobe. Remember the line from *The Devil Wears Prada* when Stanley Tucci's character exclaims, "What is that odor? Did someone here eat an onion bagel??" You don't want to be the brunt of such comments!

Portland is not very tobacco friendly, and smokers are often unaware of the sensitivity of others. If you are a smoker, be careful not to smoke in the car or wear clothes that have not been laundered.

Finally, when it comes to cologne, perfume, or strong aftershave, less is more and none is perfect. Some folks are highly sensitive to scents and you never know if one of them might be interviewing you.

YOUR STYLE IS YOUR BRAND

We've taken, once again, a fairly conventional approach to adapting your style to the style of the company in traditional interview situations. If your mustache, beard, tattoo, or stylish clothing are a part of your identity that you don't want to shed, even for an hour, we suggest that you only apply to companies where your true style is welcome—even celebrated!

You should send a thank-you message within two, no more than three, days after your interview. It can be sent either by email, LinkedIn message or, on occasion, as a card or letter—the decision should be based on the culture of the organization. A nature shot would be perfect for an interview with the Sierra Club but not for an edgy technology startup or a professional finance firm. Reiterate your enthusiasm for the position, referring to specific comments that intrigued you. If you feel that you have not fully answered a question during the interview, you can provide some follow-up information along with the thank-you.

Below is an excellent example of a thank-you letter for an interview that **Alison Wiley** had with ODOT for the State of Oregon. In effect, the letter continues the professional conversation and stresses what she can bring to the table if she is selected for the position—which she was! It's unusual to receive that kind of personal response, but this example gives you an idea of how a well-written thank-you letter with the right content can impress the desired employer.

Michael,

I greatly appreciated meeting with you and the rest of the interview panel yesterday.

Later in the afternoon, I was at a reception for Focus the Nation, where I renewed my acquaintanceship with two dynamic state legislators, Greg Macpherson and Ben Cannon. While chatting with them, I drew on what you told me about the governor's desire to make transportation a prime focus in the upcoming legislative session.

I learned that Greg is running for attorney general. If he wins he will be able to form proposals that go to the legislature, as well as have a strong hand in implementing legislation that gets passed. He seems to strongly value transportation options.

If I get the opportunity to work with you, I would continue to cultivate relationships like these in order to advance our department's transportation agendas.

Thank you again for yesterday's interview and for considering me for the position of Transportation Options Program Manager.

Sincerely,

Alison Wiley

    Hi Alison,

    Thanks for the kind words. It was my pleasure to answer your questions and provide guidance. In reality, I would have done the same for anyone that took the initiative to ask me for my input. You, however, were the only applicant to do so...and it really showed in the interviews yesterday.

    I'm not at liberty to divulge anything more, as you can understand. But it was a pleasure to have had a hand in interviewing you for an important position and I wish you all the best!

    Have a great weekend,

    Dan

Step 6
Gather Your References

"You'll never please everyone, but you only have to please a few people to get an offer." —Harvey MacKay

"Getting fired is nature's way of telling you that you had the wrong job in the first place." —Hal Lancaster

By now, you're probably getting used to the idea that most aspects of job search have changed. This applies to gathering your references as well—the way you used to do this are no longer in your best interest. Here's an overview of the old ways and their replacements:

Old way: Written letters of reference were included with your resume.

New way: Written references are part of your LinkedIn profile.

Old way: List references on your resume.

New way: Wait until they are requested, usually at the interview.

Old way: In your past company, someone in HR gave you a reference.

New way: Most of the time HR only validates dates of employment—they do not speak to your qualifications or performance.

The articles in this section show you how to make these new trends work for you:

Get Great References explains why you want to refrain from offering the names of your references until you are directly asked for them. We also give you advice on choosing your references and how to coach them to offer the most pertinent comments on your performance, targeted for a specific job.

If you had a previous bad experience with an employer, you may picture your future employer being told how you were technologically inept, wore rumpled clothing, or whatever else you can imagine when you are trying to fall asleep. In ***Bad or Iffy References***, we'll give you a road map to assess options and risks to reduce possible damage.

GET GREAT REFERENCES

When Vicki asked **Kevin**, a past client, whether he'd alerted his references to his job search, he said this: "I did indeed prepare my references. Here's why—I work hard to make the resume, cover letter, and interview the best they can be. It would be a shame if my references went poorly because they were caught unaware of my job search."

We couldn't have put it better ourselves.

At the end of his interview, Kevin contacted each reference individually to say they might receive a call from his prospective employer, but he didn't stop there; he also gave a brief overview of the organization and, if hired, what his responsibilities would be. Smart moves, but here's where Kevin earned extra points: he told his references about several of the skills and abilities that were most important to the employer—talents that he had demonstrated and cultivated while working with these contacts. He left it up to them to decide what information they would share if they received a call.

ISN'T THIS KIND OF PUSHY?

We don't think so and here's why: Let's assume that most of your references feel good about you and want to assist you in reaching your career goals. To give you a good reference, they need to be clear about the specifics of your position. If they aren't, they might, for example, focus on your wonderful flair for design when the employer is evaluating you on your technical competencies. This disconnect could hamper your chances and your references might feel responsible.

In contrast, you will shine if your references reinforce the achievements on your resume and the talking points you chose for your interview. For example, you might have stressed, both in your resume and during the interview, your collaborative nature and ability to take initiative. Such claims naturally seem more credible if your references mention them as well.

WILLING REFERENCES NEED YOUR GUIDANCE

How can you influence your references to say what you want without being too directive? First, share with them in advance some specifics about the job and the organization. Explain why you are enthusiastic about the position. Second, tactfully remind them of the pertinent projects you worked on together and the skills you used to ensure project success. In most cases, they will appreciate your guidance so that they are better prepared to give you a stellar reference.

To illustrate, here is part of a conversation Vicki had with Janet Gifford when Vicki applied for a position as a part-time coordinator of the Career Resource Center at Portland Community College.

Vicki: Hi, Janet. Will you please be one of my references for the position as a coordinator in the Career Resource Center at PCC?

Janet: I'd be glad to.

Vicki: I appreciate that. I have specifically asked you for a few reasons: first, because you reviewed my evaluations when I taught Career and Life Planning for Linfield College; and second, because this job is going to emphasize working with students of all ages

Unless you are specifically requested to do so, don't include the names and contact information of references with your resume. Very few employers check references prior to an interview anyway.

and ethnic groups. I remember when we worked together to help _____, the African-American student with a history of uneven academic success.

Janet: Oh yes, I remember seeing _____ and his father beaming when he finally made it to commencement after so many years. And you were so patient with him.

Vicki: I do miss working directly with a more diverse group of students. My private practice is wonderful, but I would like to complement it by working in a team environment. Also, I would get to teach career and planning skills like those that you hired me to teach at Linfield.

Janet: When do you expect I might receive a call?

Vicki: Within the next few days. Oh, and would you mind calling me if/when they call you? I am so enthusiastic about this—I want to know right away if they are moving forward with my candidacy.

Janet: Will do. Good luck!

TIMING IS EVERYTHING: GIVE WARNING, BUT NOT TOO MUCH

The best time to give your references a heads-up and a little subtle coaching is a few days before or after you have an interview scheduled. Send them a copy of your resume and cover letter with a brief phone or email message. For example: "I'm excited to let you know that I'm a finalist for a project manager position at Portland Purple Pickle. As you can see on my attached resume, I emphasized how the project at Green Pear came in on time and $20K below budget. I'm also pleased that this position will allow me to integrate my interest in organic foods (outside of those great company picnics we had). If you have any questions, give me a call."

RECOMMENDATIONS ON LINKEDIN

*These have become more important in this era when employers, fearing legal reprisal, often prohibit managers from discussing the strengths and weaknesses of a past employee. When you begin your job search, get in touch with those in your LinkedIn network who can offer complimentary information about your work. Ask them to endorse you for the skills required for your target job and offer to exchange recommendations. See **LinkedIn: Create an Effective Profile** for more details.*

BAD OR IFFY REFERENCES

If you have been fired or asked to resign from your last job, naturally you will have concerns about what your reference will say. You are not alone. In our career practices, we meet many wonderful, competent, and vital people who have been fired. John Fischer, a successful career changer, shared with Vicki a wonderful quote he heard during his rocky transition out of the ministry: "I wouldn't trust a person who hadn't been fired at least once in his or her life!"

Sometimes, our past positions simply weren't a good fit for us, and we might need to apply a little damage control when it comes to references. Here are five things you can do:

1. **Find out if your past employer gives references.** Most employers only verify dates of employment and eligibility for rehire. Ask your former employer's HR department about the company's references policy.

2. **If your past employer does give references**, give plenty of other references to build a balanced picture. Include other people with whom you've worked: other bosses, board members, vendors, etc.

3. **If you're filling out an application**, and you are still employed in a negative situation, it's likely you'll have to provide the name and contact information of your current supervisor.

Write "Please do not contact." The potential employer will assume that you do not want your supervisor to know that you plan to leave. This gives you more time to build a relationship with the prospective employer and emphasize your strengths.

4. **If you are no longer employed at the company**, and you must list the name of a supervisor who might criticize you, there are only two choices: include the name or write "Prefer to discuss in person." Fortunately, references are rarely contacted before the interview. The first impression you make can shape how a negative reference will be received later.

5. **Show integrity and honesty** throughout the process. Let's face it: we live in a connected world. Most hiring managers will ask their professional network about you, in addition to consulting your references. Assume that your prospective employer will find out about a conflicted relationship.

According to Pamela J. Moore, SPHR, owner of Compass Human Resources in Portland, it's better to be honest when there's been a conflict with a manager. You will present your best self, both in the interview and on the first day of a new job, if you can be open without undermining your candidacy. Describe the conflict without criticizing your ex-employer.

"I will speak with a straight tongue."
—Chief Joseph

OTHER SUCCESSFUL STRATEGIES

To get past a bad reference, several of our clients have:

- Secured a short-term contract job in the field from a supportive colleague so that the most recent reference would be from a different individual.

- Used a supportive member of the board in place of (or in addition to) the supervisor.

- Explained to the prospective employer the nature of the conflict and gave the names of three other people in the organization so they can get a fuller perspective.

- Directed the prospective employer to a large pool of positive recommendations on LinkedIn. For more information on getting LinkedIn recommendations, see *LinkedIn: Create an Effective Profile*.

- Call your iffy reference and ask them directly to share how they would address questions about your strengths and weaknesses. Listen for their content and their tone of voice to assess how they might sound when asked for actual references.

These actions might be quite emotionally demanding because they are prone to reignite the anger, sadness, or disappointment that you felt around the unhappy ending. Activate your self-care tools, from talks with supportive friends to massage therapy, when you need to address those iffy references.

 PERFORM A RANDOM ACT OF KINDNESS

Giving to others or "paying it forward" can do wonders to lift our spirits. Surprise a child with a spontaneous gift. Offer to buy a homeless person a cup of coffee or even a meal. Put together a backpack of school supplies for a disadvantaged child and take it to your neighborhood school. The possibilities for kindness are endless.

Step 7
Negotiate and Accept the Job

"Choose a job you love, and you will never have to work a day in your life." —Confucius

Wow! You've finally received a verbal job offer, with a promise of a written offer to come. It may be time for a mini celebration, maybe at Voodoo Doughnut or Yamhill Pinot Noir. You've done your job of convincing an employer that you offer the best value to help the organization reach its goal.

You might, however, want to wait before you plan your big-bang celebration; hold off until you've thoroughly followed the steps outlined in this section. This is because the way you research, negotiate, and accept a job will impact your future income and job satisfaction.

In *Salary Research* we walk you through using the best salary tools to find out where the offer falls within the range of similar positions in similar organizations. Unless the employer states otherwise, you can assume they are open to a counteroffer on compensation.

Once you are armed with salary research, an artful negotiation strategy can mean a stronger base salary, which can add up to substantial additional earnings if you stay at the company for years. In *Negotiate Your Compensation* we explain how to negotiate your entire compensation package—we help you consider if you want to make requests beyond salary regarding your job duties, benefits, vacation time, and even opportunities for remote work.

In *Is this Job Right for You?* we guide you in reviewing your job criteria one last time. Is this the right job at the right pay in the right company for you right now?

Remember the clients we introduced you to on the first pages of this handbook? In *Conclusion: Saying "Yes!"* we share their happy endings. If you peeked at this chapter before you received an offer, we hope their positive outcomes fed your optimism and perseverance.

Before you say "yes" to the job, you will want to know if the compensation package you are being offered is fair and adequate for your needs. Salary can play a large role in your overall job satisfaction for years to come, so you will want to do your research before you negotiate your pay. Here are some resources you can use for this purpose.

SALARY CALCULATORS

Begin by reviewing one of the salary calculators. Be sure to note the source of the data you find, in case you need to present it to your future employer during negotiations. Our clients rave about **Salary.com**:

I LOVED www.salary.com. So helpful, and such quality, intuitive presentation. Definitely a thumbs up. I like how the site presents things very pictorially, and graphically. The site is visually engaging and accommodating. I like how you can select different jobs that have overlap to compare them side-by-side, and I like how when you go into Salary, you can view graphs to provide you with data, and then there are different tabs you can look at that provide other useful information, such as "similar jobs," "statistics," and "job openings." —Laura Huston

Other popular sites include:

- **PayScale.com** is one of the most powerful free salary calculators on the market and is suitable for use for employees, recruiters, and reward professionals. This is because it allows you to calculate salary based on multiple criteria, including job title, country, state, city, years of experience, qualifications, and much more. This means that it will provide a far more reliable average salary figure, which makes it a stronger salary negotiation tool.

- **SalaryExpert.com** is a direct competitor to PayScale.com and shares many similarities, making it suitable for use by job seekers, recruiters, and reward professionals. Like PayScale.com, it offers an analysis based on multiple criteria including country, job title, job description/grade, and state. In addition, it offers three premium salary reports for purchase. These reports personalize your salary figure so that it is more reliable and therefore a stronger negotiation tool.

- **CBsalary.com (CareerBuilder site salary calculator)** is free and suitable for job seekers and HR professionals alike. It is powered by SalaryExpert.com and therefore offers the same functionality.

RESEARCH SIMILAR JOB POSTINGS

Another strategy is to research similar jobs that are currently posted on large national job boards such as LinkedIn and Indeed. Set the filter to list job titles above a certain compensation. If you cannot find a similar job listed locally, you can do a national search. When you locate a similar job in another part of the country you'll need to adjust for regional differences in salaries. Also, be aware that smaller companies tend to pay at the lower end of the compensation scale. Nonprofit salaries tend to run at least 25 percent lower than their counterparts in the private sector.

Tip

Don't forget about professional associations. Many include salary scales on their websites for both employment and contractor rates.

If you can't find the exact job title, search for similar or related job titles. For instance, a communications coordinator may be the equivalent of a coordinator of public relations. A vocational counselor is like a job developer; a graphic designer is similar to a commercial graphic designer; and a buyer is the equivalent of a procurement specialist.

CALL ON YOUR NETWORK

This is a great time to call on your trusted network in the field to ask their opinions. If you are hesitant about revealing the exact figure of the offer, you may want to use a range. For example:

"Hi, Claudia. I am so appreciative of your help in my job search. I am now finally in the home stretch and have been offered a position as an environmental educator for Audubon. My research has indicated that the position ought to pay within the range of ___ and the offer is lower. What is your sense of a fair salary?"

One of our clients, an environmental engineer, felt fortunate to receive a $90,000 offer from a large paper mill. She continued to dig for information and learned that some engineering companies paid a $3,000 to $5,000 signing bonus for engineers. Further research confirmed this practice, so she asked for $5,000. She got it!

Bottom Line: keep researching until you can build the most solid case for fair and deserved compensation.

BEFORE YOU START YOUR NEW JOB, TREAT YOURSELF TO A LAST-MINUTE GETAWAY.

Take in a play in Ashland or hit the big city in Seattle. If a nature getaway appeals to you, take a long weekend in Bend to go skiing at Bachelor or go horseback riding at a ranch in Wheeler county. If you like to backpack, hit the trails around The Gorge or Crater Lake. Or simply go on an overnight to the beach.

NEGOTIATE YOUR COMPENSATION

Once you've been offered a job, it's time to negotiate your salary and terms of employment. In all stages of negotiation, it is best to be positive and assertive, and support your requests with factual research.

JOB EXPECTATIONS

You want to arrive at an understanding about expectations that leaves you feeling honest and poised for success. During the interview, you may have wisely refrained from bringing up some of your concerns for fear that you might appear unenthusiastic or uncertain about your abilities. However, after an offer is extended, you can be frank about your concerns and ask for greater clarity around any implied agreements. For example, you might want to convey your confidence about three of the four desirable technical competencies but explain that you will need additional training on the fourth.

SALARY

A salary or salary range may have been posted with the initial job description. If the offer is lower than your expectations, you can make a counteroffer backed up by your research (see Salary Research). For example, one of Vicki's clients was offered a grant writing position in an environmental organization. Her research led her to believe that $62K was a fair annual salary. She was keenly disappointed when the employer offered $54K. The employer gave the rationale that another employee who had been working for two years in another job would be resentful if this client received a higher salary.

Following Vicki's guidance, her client responded by asking for a day to consider the offer. She reviewed her research and then called the next day. She told the prospective employer:

"Based on my four years of experience in the field, a master's degree, and the expectation that I will raise considerable funds, the salary offer is low."

She then provided data demonstrating that the offer was at the lowest end of expectations for someone with her job title. She asserted that the other employee probably did not have all these qualifications. She told her prospective employer that her research showed she was worth $62K to the organization and referenced the source. Then came the hardest part—she had to hold her breath for another two long days when, at last, she was offered $60K and funds to attend a desirable national conference. She concluded:

"It's too bad that it's a game, but in the end, it was worth it. Now, I can go to my first day with genuine enthusiasm."

TERMS OF EMPLOYMENT

A myriad of items can fall under this umbrella. Here are some examples:

- I have a prearranged vacation planned in October, which is six months before I would normally be eligible. The tickets are nonrefundable, and I'd like to go. Is that possible?

Did you know women are often paid less than men because they are not as aggressive at negotiating a salary commensurate with their skills and experience? Remember, your work is just as valuable, so be brave and ask for what you're worth! Easy on her ailing knees

- To effectively meet your expectations, I would need three new computers in the office. Would that be possible?

- I need to arrive at 8:30 in the morning rather than 8:00 to take my daughter to day care. Can that be arranged?

- Can I have a performance review in six months and a raise if I meet your expectations?

- Can I attend the national conference like my counterparts at Brown & Spunk Company?

Many of our clients have been successful in negotiating these types of requests before accepting the position. The employer needs to offer you some perks to be consistent with those received by other people they hired who were in a similar position. Do, however, limit your request to a few and don't expect to receive them all.

The salary and conditions you negotiate may impact your financial well-being and job satisfaction for years to come. Therefore, we highly encourage you to be thoughtful, assertive, and clear about your needs to get the job you want with the compensation package you deserve.

Tip

The negotiation process normally lasts from a day to a week, although psychologically it may seem much longer. Your job during this time is to stay in balance using proven stress reduction techniques; remember to dispel nervous energy by breathing, taking walks, and spending time with friends.

IS THIS JOB RIGHT FOR YOU?

Once you have a job offer and have negotiated your compensation, you will know your potential employer much better. If the negotiations have gone well, you may be very clear that this is the right position for you and excited to start your first day.

If you aren't entirely sold on the job, you do have one final option. Consider returning to the article *What Matters* to You to see if this position really does meet most of your criteria. Take some quiet time for introspection or a conversation with a trusted friend. Your task is to discern if your fears and doubts are normal. As they say, "Wet babies are the only ones who totally love a change."

BEV'S STORY

Bev revisited her "wish list" and remembered that she wanted a job that met these five criteria:

1. *Easy on her ailing knees*

2. *Accessible by public transportation*

3. *In a positive team environment*

4. *In higher education*

5. *Part-time so she could continue to do her artwork*

The position she was offered at the Portland State University Foundation met all her criteria except it was full-time. She had to do some soul-searching and problem solving: would she be able to keep her life as an artist alive with this job? With a mound of happiness and a pinch of sadness, she said "Yes" to the position and postponed some of her creative needs. You also need to make peace with your compromises, so you can enter the position with a heart and mind ready to greet the fresh challenges of a new job.

MIND YOUR P'S

If, after you reviewed your job criteria, you still have reservations, you may want to rate the six P's that correlate to job satisfaction.

Rate each criterion as follows:

1) Not entirely true of this position.   **2)** Generally true.   **3)** Clearly true.

CRITERIA		RATING
PURPOSE	The purpose of the organization matches your values.	
PAY	The pay and benefits are very good.	
PLACE	The drive time and quality of the location make it a good place.	
PEOPLE	You think you'll like the people who will be your coworkers.	
POSITIONING	You will gain the experience and skills, and/or meet the people to position yourself to take the next step in your career to reach your ideal.	
PLEASURE	You expect to experience pleasure in your daily activities.	
TOTAL SCORE		

Warning! A score of 12 or less raises some serious questions about your long-term satisfaction. You might want to ask your potential employer for a frank discussion—or meet in confidence with some of the other employees to address any nagging concerns. During these meetings, you can learn more about the environment by asking direct questions that you could not ask during the interview—at least not without undermining your chances of getting an offer.

Without the structure of a formal interview setting, you are likely to get the straight scoop on the upside and downside of the position. You owe it to yourself—and to your employer—to sign the contract with full anticipation of a positive, productive working relationship.

CONCLUSION: SAYING "YES!"

After reading and working through this handbook, we hope you have found your "job worth having." If you haven't yet, keep in mind there is no normal timetable to the job search adventure. The following job-changers took up to six months to land their jobs. We can all take heart from the fact that they eventually reached their destinations. You will too!

Andrea Gomez moved to LA where she successfully competed for a position which met both her financial and creative needs. She catapulted from being a poor Portland barista and photographer to becoming the new creative content producer at The Designory, a full-service marketing and advertising agency.

Nancy Banes used our process to decipher position announcements and tailor her resume to minimize the gap she took to be a homemaker and volunteer. She worked hard to update her knowledge to showcase her strengths in a series of interviews. She has now resumed her career as an environmental engineer and project manager.

Our anonymous client followed our guidelines to refine his job search strategy, tailor his resume, and improve his LinkedIn profile. Within a month he was landing interviews, and eventually successfully negotiated a job offer at a small IT company within walking distance of his home. He is thriving there as a project manager.

Laura Belson converted her volunteer work at the Metropolitan Alliance for Common Good into a part-time paid position, well matched to her role as a young mother. She has now advanced to a leadership role as the director of communications at the Industrial Area Foundation Northwest.

Mariann Hyland partnered with a career counselor, resume writer, and recruiter to win a coveted position as Vice President of People and Cultures at the Oregon Community Foundation. She is in charge of organizational development, human resources, and diversity, equity and inclusion.

Dawn Hampton found that the key to landing interviews was twofold: she had to finish the three courses she needed to get her degree and she had to submit tailored resumes. By following our suggestions for writing resumes and cover letters, she won the interview that landed her a job as a human resources assistant at Portland Mental Health.

When you say "yes" we'd love to hear about it! Maybe we can add you to our list of job search adventurers to motivate others to follow in your footsteps.

Congratulations—you've arrived!

NOW IT'S TIME FOR YOUR BIG CELEBRATION!

Take your whole support system to Ken's Artisan Pizza or maybe treat yourself to fine dining at Higgins.

NOTES